Praise for *The Personal Credibility Factor*

"The new 'PC' isn't 'political correctness'—it's 'personal credibility.' This book is a needed reminder that no matter how old you are or what you've accomplished in life, you are never, ever done learning about yourself or those around you. From the easier-said-than-done resolution to avoid gossip to the it's-as-hard-as-it-sounds process of building up your self-awareness, Allgeier has filled her book with the life lessons we never seem to fully learn the first time we hear them. (Or maybe that's just me!)"

—**Mike Staver**, CEO of The Staver Group;
author of *Do You Know How to Shut Up? And 51 Other Life Lessons That Will Make You Uncomfortable*

"To be an effective leader, you *must* be trustworthy. If people don't trust you, they won't follow you. And if they won't follow you, your organization won't meet its goals. Sandy Allgeier explains that personal credibility comes down to a simple truth: It's not about the type of person you *are*; it's about the types of things you *do*. If you want to be a great leader, read *The Personal Credibility Factor*."

—**Quint Studer**, CEO and founder of Studer Group®;
bestselling author of *Results That Last: Hardwiring Behaviors That Will Take Your Company to the Top* and *Hardwiring Excellence: Purpose, Worthwhile Work, Making a Difference*

"Personal credibility has everything to do with how others perceive us and how we perceive ourselves. Sandy Allgeier's book teaches the all-important truth that it doesn't matter how much money, status, or power you have if nobody believes in you. Every parent should read *The Personal Credibility Factor* and instill its lessons in their kids. Achieving a full understanding of these principles is the first step in becoming a truly great human being."

—**Michele Borba**, Ed.D., internationally renowned educator;
award-winning author of 21 books including *12 Simple Secrets Real Moms Know: Getting Back to Basics and Raising Happy Kids; Nobody Likes Me, Everybody Hates Me!; and No More Misbehavin': 38 Difficult Behaviors and How to Stop Them*

"Sandy Allgeier succinctly conveys how critical it is to earn the respect of those around you. It's true: Being respected propels you forward in life like nothing else. And all is not lost when you make a mistake—Allgeier includes a much-appreciated chapter on how we can win back personal credibility when we've faltered. *The Personal Credibility Factor* will teach anyone who reads it how to become a better, more authentic, more successful human being."

—**Dr. Nido R. Qubein**, President, High Point University;
Chairman, Great Harvest Bread Co.

"Between these covers lies the stuff great organizations are made of. If you're a business owner or leader, I suggest you make *The Personal Credibility Factor* required reading for your employees and yourself. You'll learn the importance of authenticity, of transparency, of asking yourself on a daily basis if you're striving to be the best person you can be. If everyone in your organization reads this book, not only will it be a better place to work, but I guarantee you your customers will be happier, too."

—**Jeffrey A. Miller**, CEO of Jeffrey Miller + Associates;
author of *The Anxious Organization: Why Smart Companies Do Dumb Things*

P9-CBJ-149

"I found myself nodding in agreement as I turned the pages of *The Personal Credibility Factor*. It proves the lesson I learned as a child—one I now pass on to my students—is true: Your actions *do* speak louder than your words. Sandy Allgeier's book spells out the basics of building personal credibility in an eloquent, readable way. In fact, I plan to start recommending it to my students and their parents!"

—**Tom Bloch**, former CEO of H&R Block;
currently a middle school math teacher, board president, and cofounder of University
Academy; author of *Stand for the Best: What I Learned after Leaving My Job as CEO of
H&R Block to Become a Teacher and Founder of an Inner-City Charter School*

"Personal credibility is a key factor for success in any organization. The ability of HR professionals to assess the presence or absence of this quality in others is critical. Filling an organization with people who score high in personal credibility should be the goal of everyone in the field. This book will teach you how!"

—**Barbara Sadek**, Director of Education,
Society for Human Resource Management

"I've learned over the years that there is no greater asset than personal credibility. Ms. Allgeier wonderfully conveys that lesson in her great new book! Whether you're just starting out or have been working for decades, read this book and watch your career and your life improve exponentially. It's never too late."

—**Mike Sims**, Senior Principal,
High Point Partners

"Sandy Allgeier is the poster child for personal credibility! She not only lives it and breathes it, but she also teaches it and communicates its principles effectively to audiences of all kinds. Her high energy, confident style, and warmth engage her audiences, enabling them to change their behaviors and make a difference in their work lives and personal lives. Her new book is bound to be a classic found on every manager's and employee's bookshelf."

—**Cathy Fyock**, CSP, SPHR, consultant, author,
Resources Global Professionals

"Whether it's advice on how to interact with others or insights on how to evaluate your own personal credibility, Sandy Allgeier delivers. As a leader in business and now in the college classroom, I know that I can be effective only if those I lead think highly of me. This excellent book validates that truth."

—**Elaine Robinson**, Executive in Residence, University of Louisville College of Business;
formerly Vice President and Treasurer,
Providian Corporation

"*The Personal Credibility Factor* is filled with practical advice about how to improve the most important resource we possess—our credibility. Whether you want to hone your business skills or enhance your personal relationships, Sandy Allgeier helps you examine yourself and create a personal game plan to improve. I hope everyone who reads her book will be inspired to become more influential, more authentic, and more trustworthy human beings."

—**Gregg Dedrick**, President,
KFC Corp.

THE PERSONAL CREDIBILITY FACTOR

How to Get It, Keep It,
and Get It Back,
(If You've Lost It)

Sandy Allgeier

Vice President, Publisher: Tim Moore
Associate Publisher and Director of Marketing: Amy Neidlinger
Acquisitions Editor: Jennifer Simon
Editorial Assistant: Myesha Graham
Development Editor: Russ Hall
Operations Manager: Gina Kanouse
Digital Marketing Manager: Julie Phifer
Publicity Manager: Laura Czaja
Assistant Marketing Manager: Megan Colvin
Cover Designer: Chuti Prasertsith
Managing Editor: Kristy Hart
Project Editor: Anne Goebel
Copy Editor: Karen Annett
Senior Compositor/Interior Designer: Gloria Schurick
Manufacturing Buyer: Dan Uhrig

FT Press offers excellent discounts on this book when ordered in quantity for bulk purchases
or special sales. For more information, please contact U.S. Corporate and Government Sales,
1-800-382-3419, corpsales@pearsontechgroup.com. For sales outside the U.S., please contact
International Sales at international@pearsoned.com.

First Printing February 2009

ISBN-10: 0-13-208279-9
ISBN-13: 978-0-13-208279-2

Pearson Education LTD.
Pearson Education Australia PTY, Limited.
Pearson Education Singapore, Pte. Ltd.
Pearson Education North Asia, Ltd.
Pearson Education Canada, Ltd.
Pearson Educatión de Mexico, S.A. de C.V.
Pearson Education—Japan
Pearson Education Malaysia, Pte. Ltd.

Library of Congress Cataloging-in-Publication Data

Allgeier, Sandy
    The personal credibility factor / Sandy Allgeier.
        p. cm.
    ISBN 0-13-208279-9 (pbk. : alk. paper) 1. Respect for persons. 2. Self-esteem. I. Title.
    BJ1533.R42A45 2009
    170'.44—dc22
                                2008007863

Contents

CONTENTS

Application Exercises:

Acknowledgments

I have always thought authors were cut from a different cloth—one very different from which I was cut! For years, I have been advised by friends and associates to write a book. For years, my immediate response was, "I don't think so!" That changed in 2007. After training and speaking to groups for years on the topic of personal credibility, I was invited to write a book about it. After working through my own doubts about writing, I decided to try it. Beverly Sills, the now deceased and famous opera star, once said, "I would rather die saying that I probably shouldn't have tried something, than die wishing I had!" I have now tried it and feel so blessed to have had the opportunity.

Special thanks go to Jennifer Simon. Jen, thanks so much for seeking *me* out of the many new and established authors who come across your path. You simply instilled me with the confidence I needed to get this going.

My husband, Rick, both encouraged me and allowed me to work in a way that provided "safety"—just in case I learned that I couldn't write very well! Rick is the most credible human being I have ever had the opportunity to know.

My colleague and friend, Heather Gates, allowed me the opportunity to crystallize my thoughts and create a starting place.

My many friends have been such strong sources of encouragement. In particular, Cathy Fyock and Mike Sims were ongoing cheerleaders, encouragers, or kick-my-tail'ers—dishing out whatever I needed, whenever that might be.

My parents are proud of me, but I am most proud to be their daughter. They taught me the value of personal credibility and are still teaching me. I can only pray that I'll leave that kind of legacy with my own children and grandchildren.

Thanks most of all to God. He must have wanted me to write about this topic because He opened every door to make it happen. I just hope this work can somehow glorify Him!

About the Author

Sandy Allgeier, SPHR, is a speaker, consultant, trainer/facilitator, and coach who helps organizations maximize their human resource potential. Before launching her consulting business in 2000, she had 25+ years' experience in HR, rising to SVP of HR at a major provider of assisted living services, with responsibility for over 7,000 employees.

Allgeier contributed to the book *Conversations on Success, Volume 7* (Insight, 2005), which also featured Stephen Covey and Dr. Denis Waitley. She earned the 1999 Award for Professional Excellence from SHRM's Louisville, Kentucky chapter and was selected as faculty member and facilitator for SHRM's HR Generalist Certificate and Recruitment and Retention Certificate Programs.

Introduction

I Wouldn't Trust That Person for a Minute!

You have probably had this feeling before. It's that little mental nudge you get when you really don't expect it. It might even seem somewhat irrational at the time. Try to put yourself in the following situation: You have been invited to have lunch with a respected business consultant who is interested in hiring you as a contractor. "Kate" has a solid reputation and an established consulting business. She wants you to consider joining her as a consulting partner to work with some of her best clients, and this could mean wonderful earning potential for you! The lunch is going well—but you cannot shake this odd feeling that something just isn't right. That little voice will not go away that is saying, "Don't trust! Eat your lunch and let it go at that. This just doesn't feel right!"

Or perhaps the opposite has happened to you—which might be equally confounding. Have you ever been challenged with hiring contractors to help you with projects around your house? Most of us have learned that hiring someone for odd jobs, such as small building projects or fixing a clogged drain, can be downright infuriating. Perhaps you have experienced the frustration of having a contractor who won't return your phone calls. Or, maybe you can identify with the challenges of having appointments made to estimate pricing, but no one shows up. Then, when you call to find out what happened—your call isn't returned. Unfortunately, you begin to believe that you will never be able to find someone to do the work.

Then, amazingly, someone walks into your life that is dramatically different. If you are fortunate enough, you meet someone like "Dan." Even though you are a little cynical about hiring contractors, you believe that Dan will keep his appointments, follow through on commitments, and do a great job with anything he agrees to do. And, he won't agree to do something that he doesn't believe he can do effectively. When you look back on it, you can remember being certain that Dan could be trusted from the first time you talked with him.

So, what does this mean? Does it mean that most of us have internal voices that can predict whether someone is trustworthy and credible? Does this mean that personal credibility is just something we instinctively sense in others? And, what about you? Do others instinctively believe and trust in you—or is there some reason that others are naturally skeptical of you?

Our "instincts" about people can be helpful, but, obviously, it is so much more than that.

It isn't particularly complicated either. Everyone can have strong personal credibility—but it does require that we understand it, desire it, and make a decision to seek it for our lives.

What Is the Personal Credibility Factor?

When others believe, trust, and have confidence in you, you naturally receive their respect—you are someone with *personal credibility*. When you are respected, your self-worth and confidence increases. When you receive respect—from both yourself and others—you are more self-accepting. Self-acceptance allows you to just be yourself, which increases authenticity. When you are authentic, others instinctively believe and trust in you more.

But wait…Is personal credibility based on the type of person that *you are*, or is it based on the types of things that *you do*?

If you really think about it, the only way we can assess people is from our observations of what they do.

It is what people do that forms our opinions, relationships, and ultimate decisions of whether to trust and respect them. Our impressions, thoughts, and opinions are constantly being formed and re-formed, most often in our subconscious. Although we might be unaware of it, we stay in constant "observer" mode with those around us, and they stay in that same mode observing us! We might not always have all the facts, and our observations might change over time, but, regardless, it is still the only information on which we have to base our thoughts and opinions of others. For this reason, it is what people *do* that determines our belief, respect, and trust in them—it is what we all *do* that determines personal credibility.

Why would this matter? It's really pretty simple. At our very core, we want to know who we can trust and respect—and we want to receive that same trust and respect from others. However, we are living in a world where it is becoming more and more difficult to discern who deserves our trust and respect. Headlines and TV news are filled regularly with stories of troubled organizations such as WorldCom and Enron, fallen TV evangelists, government leaders, and others taking the spotlight for misleading the public. Consequently, we find ourselves wondering if personal credibility with public figures is only something of the past. On a more personal level, family, friends, or coworkers violate our trust and lose credibility as a result. Most people—regardless of whether they are in the public spotlight—don't intentionally choose a life of being disbelieved, mistrusted, and disrespected.

The reality is that personal credibility either occurs or is damaged due to ongoing decisions we make and behaviors we demonstrate.

For most of us, there is an inherent need to be valued and respected by others, while at the same time, to be comfortable and confident in being who we authentically are. We want to live a life that causes others to say: "(Your name)—now that is someone with personal credibility!" We all don't experience that type of life though. The great news is this: We can experience greater personal credibility—if we are willing to honestly evaluate ourselves, look at our own actions and behaviors, and build some new habits.

Part I

The Three Secrets to Personal Credibility

Tell Everyone: There Are Actually **Three** Secrets!

Regardless of where you are in your life—successful or struggling, just starting out or moving into your later years, thrilled with your life or wrestling with discontent—you can be positively impacted by the information you will read about increasing your own personal credibility. The three secrets are not meant to be locked up but shared with everyone!

Why is personal credibility so important? What is its value?

When people have strong personal credibility, they are able to inspire others to trust and believe in who they are and what they do. Strong personal credibility helps us to create productive relationships with others and to accomplish more within those relationships. Creating and maintaining relationships is a critical factor in both our personal and professional lives. It really doesn't matter whether we are discussing our relationships with our friends, kids, parents, siblings, employees, or leaders. With greater personal credibility, others trust us. When trust is strong, we experience fewer barriers in relationships. When relationship barriers are decreased, we accomplish more and enjoy what we do. With lesser personal credibility, others are more distrusting, causing us to fight ongoing, uphill battles in every aspect of our lives.

The Personal Credibility Factor: What is yours and why should you care? Personal credibility is about respect, trust, and about being believable…but what builds it? And what tears it down? Can you have it and lose it? And, if you lose it, can you get it back? Is there a difference between being simply trustworthy and being a person of high personal credibility? Lots of questions—how about a few answers, huh?

First, start by understanding three simple secrets that can help any of us increase our own personal credibility factor. After you understand these, you can then make the choice to evaluate your own habits and behaviors and seize the opportunity to increase your personal credibility.

Reading for All It's Worth...

Just reading this book will likely give you some new insights into your daily life experiences and how you personally build or lose credibility as a result of what you do and how you do it. Most of us find, however, that gaining insight doesn't necessarily get us to the point of taking specific *actions* that can positively change our lives. *Actions* require exactly that—thought, movement, and action on what we learn! As you read—take some action! Pick up your pen or pencil, make notes, underline and highlight anything that speaks to you in a personal way. And, take the small amount of time needed to work through the simple yet important exercises that are provided throughout. You'll find that the insight you gain will be much deeper and, most important, you'll move from *learning* more about this topic to *doing* what it takes to enhance your own personal credibility.

chapter one

Secret #1:
Forget Power, Position, Status, and Other Such Nonsense

Strong personal credibility is available for everyone—regardless of who you are and what you do. Your position, status, or role in life have nothing to do with your personal credibility factor. Different people play different roles in their careers, jobs, and other activities—and some are roles of very high authority—however, there's no lasting connection between higher status/power and personal credibility. Let's look at a few examples.

Same Ideas, But Very Different Results

"John" held a senior vice president position in a large Fortune 500 organization. John was a creative, likable, and bright executive. His staff and peers greatly enjoyed working with him and he inspired others to new and creative ways of thinking. As a member of the senior leadership team, John regularly presented suggestions, recommendations, and proposals for consideration with his fellow senior leaders. Unfortunately, the outcome of most of those recommendations was, "Uh, good idea, John. But we can't implement that idea right now. Maybe we can reconsider later." He was politely listened to and verbally patted on the head. John just did not have a good track record for gaining approval for his ideas.

This organization was growing, and as is customary when companies grow quickly, reorganization became necessary. "Alice," another member of the senior management team, was asked to assume responsibility for a larger role in leadership, and as a result, John, along with two other colleagues, was now to report to Alice in her new role as chief administrative officer. John respected Alice and accepted this restructuring positively.

Then, an odd thing started to happen to John's ideas and recommendations. Alice reviewed many of them personally and then worked with John and the other senior leaders to reconsider implementing those ideas. In about six weeks, approximately 80 percent of the recommendations John had previously made were funded and approved by the president and the other members of the leadership team. These were the same ideas that did not receive much positive attention previously. Why? Alice had personal credibility. John simply did not have it—or at least at the same level. Although John was liked, he did not have the strong respect of the other leaders. In Alice's new position, she worked with John to have his ideas reevaluated and considered. Although the authority within John's position was the same, under Alice's leadership, the results were very different. You might be thinking that since Alice now had more authority within her newly established position that she was able to get more accomplished.

Bigger position—greater power, right?

Actually, that had no real impact in this situation. The people on the leadership team who had shot down John's ideas were the same people who later approved them. Alice held the same "rank" as the rest of the members of this team, no more or less positional power than others who were involved in the decision making. This group of leaders, however, believed that Alice would not make recommendations unless they were solid. They just did not have the same confidence in John. We'll explore more about the specifics that impacted that later. But, the key point is that results did not occur as a result of the *position* Alice or John were in. Both of their positions had status and authority, but Alice was respected—she had stronger personal credibility. Naturally, John was mystified by Alice's results and why they differed so much from his own. Why did Alice get more respect from the leadership team? Why did it matter that *she* was recommending the same basic concepts that he had previously and yet she received approval? Eventually, John asked Alice to explain how she was able to gain such different outcomes. At first, Alice wasn't sure how to respond to John's question. She needed to spend some time thinking about what she did and how she did it. Eventually, however, she was able to provide John with some very specific feedback about how she had learned to work hard in a few basic areas, and how that work had paid off for her. She realized she had learned to do certain things that would increase her opportunity to gain others' trust and respect. She also assured John that he could choose to make a few simple changes that could significantly improve his results as well. In later chapters, you will discover more about Alice and what she did—and what John had been doing that was diminishing his success and decreasing his personal credibility with this team.

It's What You **Do**, Not What You **Say**

"Chuck" was a leader in a large call center operation. He was bright, tough-minded, and very strongly opinionated. He spoke with authority, and those working with him had no doubt that he would take action based on that authority. He also had a tendency to be somewhat lazy. It was not unusual to see Chuck reclined at his desk, feet up, reading *The Wall Street Journal*. Chuck met periodically with his leadership team, told them his expectations, and then verbally blasted those whose results were less than expected. The performance of Chuck's team was pretty strong—for a while. Then, performance began to suffer. His team of leaders slowly but surely were either seeking positions elsewhere or were very busy trying to find ways to keep Chuck's attention off them. Eventually, Chuck's business results decreased significantly, and this ended in his being replaced.

"Mitch" replaced Chuck. Mitch was also bright and strongly opinionated. Like Chuck, Mitch told people exactly what he thought and expected. He regularly had informal "floor meetings" where he walked from area to area, brought small groups together, told them what he wanted for the organization, and gave time for them to ask questions and make suggestions. He listened respectfully, considered others' perspectives, and kept employees informed with information on his future plans. He didn't attempt to make everyone happy—but he usually explained the reasons for his actions and for decisions he made. Mitch also demonstrated energy and passion for his job and the business. If he wasn't out on the floor talking with people, he was meeting regularly with individual leaders to brainstorm ideas for improvement. Not surprisingly, it was fairly common to hear employees in the organization speak about the difference in leadership styles between Chuck and Mitch. Interestingly, the terms "say" and "do" were used to describe both leaders. Chuck was often referred to as "Mr. Do as I Say, Not as I Do." The managers who reported to him often rolled their eyes when leaving conversations with Chuck, incredulous with how he spent his time reading the newspaper while at the same time verbally assaulting them for failing to give enough effort to achieve better results. Mitch, by contrast, was referred to as a leader who would not ask anyone to do anything he wasn't willing to do first. Employees knew where both leaders stood on issues. They also learned that only one of the leaders, Mitch, was willing to stand in the same place he was asking others to stand. As a result, Mitch was able to gain employees' willingness to accept and trust his direction.

The organization under Mitch's leadership began to show more positive results. The business improved. The parent company decided to use this location as a testing ground for new products and processes. Think about it...Chuck and Mitch had the same degree of "position authority." These two people held the same job with the same power within the position. The results were very different—but it wasn't the power or authority of the *role* that made the difference! The difference was in how they behaved—and as a result, Mitch gained respect, whereas Chuck lost it.

Secret #1 Applies to Other Life Experiences

We just reviewed two business leadership examples. But what about comparing status or position in our personal lives? We see examples of it every day—with parents, teachers, or even staff at our local coffee shops. The Starbucks barista has less authority within his/her position than the store manager. If you occasionally visit coffee shops, you understand that after you are known as a "regular," you are hoping to interact with the person who connects with you, remembers your favorite drink in the morning—versus the afternoon—and makes some type of comment that makes you feel recognized or special. You are not at all concerned about whether you are dealing with the manager—you just want to interact with the person who has proven credibility and who you trust to know your preferences! The real power is the positive impact this person leaves as you walk or drive away!

School principals have more authority within their organizations than teachers. When it comes to your kids and how they are performing in school, do you think first about the highest authority position to deal with, or do you think about talking with the individual teacher who is interacting with your child? Typically, the person you want to talk with is the person who has the greatest influence on your child's situation—the teacher!

Power and authority are not the issue!

Credibility in Parenting

"Charles" and "Linda" are the parents of two young children. They're a typical young family; both parents work, with precious little time to themselves and with the demands of a four- and two-year-old, plus balancing the rest of their hectic lives—they can feel pretty stressed at times. Occasionally, they lose patience with their kids, and occasionally, they give in to the demands those kiddos place upon them. Generally, though, they treat parenting as their top priority. They make mistakes, like we all do. But, they send very strong messages to their children that they are loved, and that they as parents will set the rules and boundaries for their lives on a daily, consistent basis. Their children are delightful to be around.

"Susan" and "Steve" are also parents. Their children have been raised in very similar circumstances regarding schedules, working parents, and so on. Unfortunately, though, Susan and Steve have raised their children as an afterthought. It's sad, but in reality, it is true. They were not ready to take on the responsibility of raising kids.

A typical day in the lives of Susan, Steve, and their kids goes something like this:

Kid says:	*"I want to go to the school roller skating party on Friday night."*
Parent says:	*"We'll talk about it later."*
Kid says (next day):	*"I want to go to the roller skating party Friday night."*
Parent says:	*"I told you...we will talk about it later!"*

Friday night arrives, and the kid is demanding to go. The parents, after all the nondiscussions, are resisting. The kid has a temper tantrum. And...the punishment for the tantrum is:

"You WILL NOT go anywhere tonight or all weekend because of your behavior!"

No one enjoys being around Susan and Steve with their children. It is always a scene of loud disagreement, and the children are becoming sulkier and more difficult in general.

The difference here? Personal credibility. Charles and Linda have established it with their children. Their kids are learning that their parents will behave in a certain way that they can rely on and trust. Susan and Steve have lost credibility and, unfortunately, don't even realize it. Their children don't know if they will be ignored, punished, or even indulged because their parents don't want to deal with the pressure the kids place on them. Steve and Susan just know they are extremely stressed and have children who are likely to have meltdowns. The status or power of being a parent doesn't mean anything—both sets of parents have the power of the position of parent—it is the parents' credibility (or lack of it) that leaves the impact on children and others.

> *Think about your life. How much of your effectiveness as a parent, employee, leader, spouse, friend, volunteer—whatever role you are playing—occurs as a result of the power or status of your position?*

Honestly answer the following questions. Be sure to consider both your professional and work situations as you do.

1. Why do others respond positively to me when I request something from them?

    In my personal life:

    _____

    In my work life:

    _____

2. If I had no authority to give direction, how likely is it that others would choose to respond positively to my direction?

    In my personal life:

    _____

    In my work life:

    _____

If your responses to these two questions indicate that you rely heavily upon the power, status, or position of the role you are in, you might want to think about that. If you are dependent upon "because I said so" to accomplish results in any part of your life, just think about it and how that might be impacting your personal credibility. Although position or status might help you gain short-term results or superficial respect from others, it rarely sustains for long periods of time. People who establish and maintain strong personal credibility have come to understand that their personal credibility factor is based on what they do—not the position or role that they have.

chapter two

Secret #2:
I Can See Right Through You

You might be a pet owner or know one. Most of us who have been around pets in urban or suburban areas are familiar with invisible fences. The little dog comes outside, runs around the perimeter of the yard, and might bark like crazy when someone passes by. The invisible fence, combined with the collar the dog is wearing, keeps the dog safely inside the yard. The dog stays safe from passing vehicles; the neighbors stay safe from a possible dog bite. All is well!

The Human Invisible Fence

People can have invisible fences, too. Just as with an invisible pet fence, we cannot see the invisible fence someone might place around himself, but the presence of the fence can greatly impact what happens when we interact with the person who has the fence activated. Most of us even have a built-in alarm that sounds when we sense the other person has the invisible fence activated!

Authenticity: We Know It When It's Not There

Think about someone you have known who has had a tendency to brag or enlarge the truth on a regular basis. This person, over time, loses credibility with you. Usually, this person is someone you would not describe as authentic or real. Over time, you are likely to lose trust in anything this person says. Indeed, this person will definitely lose personal credibility as a result of this behavior. What is going on with this person? Well, it's likely this person has erected a very strong invisible fence. She wants others to see her in a way that is different than what she really believes about herself. Typically, her self-image is usually negative for some reason. Eventually, your reaction will be, "If you can't be sincere and honest in what you say or how you share information, I can't trust you. You brag and enlarge the truth. You aren't for real. And If I can't trust you, I don't want a close relationship with you." Ultimately, this person has lost personal credibility because she has lost your trust.

Or consider others you have known who are very stiff or stilted in their communication with you. It's difficult to get a sense of who this person really is. This individual is likely to open up very little to anyone and reveals little about himself. He keeps everyone at arm's length—almost as if there is a wall surrounding him. He keeps most everyone *outside* his invisible fence. The result is that others find it difficult to trust someone who is so unwilling to demonstrate openness and authenticity. The invisible fence this person has activated creates a distance with others, decreases trust, and, ultimately, decreases the opportunity for this person to build trusting relationships with him. Others will simply say, "If you don't trust me enough to be sincere and open, I really can't trust you either." Without trust from others, this individual loses personal credibility.

Personal credibility is dependent upon the ability to inspire trust and respect in others.

When someone behaves in a way that makes sense to us and inspires us to trust him or her as being authentic and real, that person increases personal credibility. And the opposite is true as well. When we interact with someone who is unwilling or unable to be sincere and authentic, we lose trust. In our eyes, that person loses personal credibility. It's a trust thing!

When something is transparent, we can see through it. Nothing is hidden, no barriers exist, and nothing is covered up. When *someone* is transparent, we know that we are seeing the "true" person. But, transparency is more than being truthful—it is being truthful in a way that others can easily detect. When someone is transparent, and clearly demonstrates behaviors that others value and trust, personal credibility is much more easily achieved. This person is believable—is secure enough in his/her own skin to put up no "fronts" or masks. However, when those barriers are in place, it is as if the person has an invisible fence around him. Although we can't visually see the fence, most of us sense it immediately. The opportunity to be transparent and authentic is there for every human on Earth. It does require that we examine our own invisible fences—and then decide if we can or should deactivate them.

The Silent Alarm System

Most of us have a certain degree of intuition about other people. Think of it as your HIFA (Human Invisible Fence Antennae)—your ability to interact with someone briefly and determine this person's sincerity, authenticity, and comfort with simply being themselves. (There is a more commonly used term that might be more familiar: your bullsh__ detector!) When you interact, your subconscious is busy determining if this person is being real—or if there is some type of barrier that causes you to question the individual's believability. When your "HIFA" alarm sounds, you might not know why, you just know it is there. You might have sensed this alarm when someone is "putting up a front," which we usually sense as someone being phony or when we sense that someone is closing themselves off or hiding something. Either way, most of us sense that invisible fence pretty quickly.

What is this invisible fence and where does it come from?
All of us have one—we just engage it differently
based on our circumstances!

When someone has activated his or her protective invisible fence, it is much more difficult to accurately read this person. You can somehow sense that he or she is protecting or distancing their true self for some reason. That person might just have the fence activated temporarily or it might be more of a permanent fixture.

It All Begins with Accepting Our Own Human Warts

Individuals who possess strong personal credibility have an authenticity about them that is detectable. The invisible fence doesn't seem to exist. No alarm sounds when we interact with this person. They give an "I am who I am" impression to others. Typically, the more transparent people are, the less inclined they are at *trying* to impress others. Now, this doesn't mean they don't care about others or the impact they have on them—quite the opposite. It means simply that the focus is not on, "What are you thinking of *me*?" but instead on, "How can I better know and understand *you*?"

Individuals who are transparent in a positive and genuine way are typically self-accepting. They understand that they are imperfect beings. They know they mess up, make mistakes, and don't have all the answers. They are strong enough to accept this, and then go about the process of living their life by internally acknowledging imperfections and challenges—and learning from them. They expect others to make mistakes, too. As a result, there is no real need to activate the invisible fence, but rather a need to identify the mistake, learn the lesson, and then move on. We demonstrate our own self-acceptance through our willingness to develop and practice respectful yet open, honest, and straightforward communication processes. We'll explore all sorts of ways later in the book to achieve that type of communication and, as a result, increase the opportunity for increased personal credibility.

This might be one of the more difficult to understand—as well as difficult to change—areas of personal credibility. Those invisible fences have often been in place for a long time, sometimes a lifetime, and they feel so much a part of us that we honestly don't even realize they are there. And, there could be a million reasons—often very legitimate ones—that someone has chosen to activate the fence to protect something about himself.

Typically, we build our fences when we lack confidence for some reason.

When we activate our invisible fence, we begin to *act in a way that we believe is either more acceptable to others or one that we perceive to be safe*—versus being our true and imperfect selves. We learn to trade in our *authenticity* for *acting* because we convince ourselves that our act is more acceptable.

Invisible Fences Don't All Look Alike

The invisible fence can activate in a variety of ways. A very successful business entrepreneur, "Pete," is extremely engaging when interacting with others. He is sociable, humorous, and has very persuasive communication skills. When first meeting Pete, most people react quickly with, "What a great guy!" He is gifted at remembering a few facts about everyone and is impressive with his ability to recall names and facts about people for years! Over time, though, people who know him do not describe Pete as being authentic or transparent. Instead, he tends to send a signal of, "Watch out—I have some ulterior motive for my behavior." After learning more about Pete, many realize that he is inclined to make cruel comments about others behind their backs while simultaneously building their egos to their faces. Those around Pete eventually lose trust in him because he is acting as if he is genuinely interested in others, but his behavior suggests the opposite. Ultimately, others realize that Pete does not demonstrate authenticity—and he loses trust from others.

"Donna" also activates her invisible fence—but in a different way. While her parents and siblings are very close-knit, she just doesn't feel like she is accepted within her family. So, she stays very distant, only seeing her family at major holidays such as Thanksgiving and Christmas. She is invited to attend all family functions, but she doesn't enjoy being there, and she usually declines invitations. Donna's family members can sense her invisible fence when she enters a room—it is almost as if it sends off tiny shock waves. In truth, the family is simply reacting to Donna's actions when she's around them. She is very detached, and her body language communicates her discomfort. She barely speaks unless making sarcastic remarks, gives stiff, almost perfunctory hello and goodbye hugs, and leaves these gatherings as quickly as she possibly can. Donna doesn't share her thoughts and feelings with her family. She's keeping a lot closed in behind that invisible fence—and her family sees only someone who is always critical, stiff, and distant—never truly open or authentic! Donna's personal credibility has been impaired with her family for several other reasons that we'll discuss later. For now, just understand that she is extremely guarded with her family and shares virtually nothing about herself. Her invisible fence seems nearly impenetrable.

What do Pete and Donna have in common? Certainly at least one thing: Both are behaving in a way that causes others to have distrust because there is a lack of genuine *authenticity*. Pete behaves in a way that he thinks will cause others to accept him. He compliments others, builds them up to their face, and *acts* like he believes others are important. But he then destroys the respect he is trying to gain when he frequently behaves in the opposite manner by demeaning others in comments and actions behind their backs. Pete believes he is gaining others' respect, but the opposite is true.

Donna, who we will explore further in future chapters, has made many, many mistakes in her interactions with her family. But, rather than accepting and acknowledging her mistakes, even to herself, she keeps her family distanced from her physically and emotionally. She shares nothing about her life, she connects only when she feels she must, she is distant and cold, and, therefore, family members have no basis for trusting her. Their reaction is, "If all you give is criticism and a cold shoulder to us, how can we know who you really are and what you really think? How can we trust you?"

"Nellie" has seven siblings—three "natural" siblings and four "step" siblings. The family "blending" occurred when the eight children were between the ages of 16 and 22. Now, the brothers and sisters are in their fifties. Nellie is the youngest. Today, all eight enjoy each other and manage to get together as a family periodically, even though their parents are deceased. Like most families, this one is spread across the country and it's difficult to remain close. Nellie, however, has somehow maintained her close relationship with all her siblings—both natural and step. When you ask the family to describe Nellie, the first thing you hear is, "She is the most genuine and authentic person I know." If Nellie has an invisible fence, no one has ever sensed it. Her authenticity and confidence is what shines through. She is filled with joy and laughter, but she also has the same challenges with sadness, frustration, and anger as anyone else. She's just someone who is always the genuine, real, human being—no matter what! Regardless of the relationship between others in her family, each sibling easily reaches out to Nellie and has a close, meaningful relationship with her.

Pete has an active invisible fence; he wants others to believe he is sincere and cares about them, but his actions indicate this is not so. Donna's invisible fence keeps her from interacting openly with her family, causing both Donna and her family to miss out on any type of meaningful relationship with her. Pete and Donna are acting—and others pick up on this act, and the HIFA alarm sounds. Nellie, on the other hand, is seen by all who know her as being open, approachable, and someone with total authenticity.

Authentic Results, Even During Tough Times

Most of us tend to keep our invisible fences deactivated when we are totally at ease and feel accepted by others. The true measure of being authentic is when we are authentic even in difficult situations. "Rob" was the president of a business unit of a large financial services organization. Only six months after joining the organization, Rob was informed that the business was going to be purchased by a large organization based in Europe. Rob had just uprooted his family and his life when moving from his prior role in a successful business located in Chicago to take this role in the southeastern United States. He was informed by the board that it was possible for his business unit to remain in place, for his role with the business to remain the same— but it was highly unlikely. It was more likely that the business would relocate to Europe, and his role as president would be eliminated. Rob was informed that he would participate as a member of a transition team to help make that determination, and he was also told to "hold things together" during this very difficult, uncertain time for the organization.

Rob knew what "hold things together" meant: He needed to keep people focused and keep the business running successfully. Rob also had absolute insight into Secret #1: He fully believed that he could not achieve these results as a result of his "position" of president. He knew his greatest risk was losing valuable organizational talent and, as a result, experience declining performance. Why would employees make decisions to stay with the organization and perform well just because "the president said so"? He knew that people needed honesty and respect from a leader. Rob believed the way he could gain the respect of the 700+ employees was to be genuine, authentic, and respectful of them.

Rob began holding short "lobby talks" to update employees on the status of the acquisition and the results of the work being done by the transition team. He made statements like:

> *"I can honestly tell you that I don't know where this business will be located or who will lead it. I will absolutely tell you, however, that I will keep you informed as I learn more."*

He also said:

> *"I'm sure you are struggling with the uncertainty of this situation. I know, it is a struggle for me, too."*

Or:

> *"I know that I have trouble falling asleep some nights, and I'm sure that you have the same problem."*

He didn't hide his personal concerns, but he also helped employees see the options that might be available for them even if the company did relocate. He did not promise anything, but instead helped employees fully understand what was occurring. He asked for employee commitment and performance during this difficult time— and he committed to doing everything he could do to help them by providing ongoing and honest information.

Interestingly, other business units of the same organization began to hear about the "lobby talks" that were occurring in Rob's part of the business. Employees who worked in other business units began to show up during the lobby talks, even though they worked in different locations and buildings across town. Many stated that Rob's lobby talks were the only information they were able to learn about the upcoming acquisition as their own business unit leaders were not communicating about the status of the activities. In just a few weeks, the lobby talks were dubbed "Robby in the Lobby" by employees who crowded into the lobby of the building just to hear what was happening.

In addition to the need for information, these employees were also drawn to Rob's *authenticity* as a leader. They wanted to hear the truth—from someone who was concerned enough about everyone to share the truth in an open, thoughtful way. The truth was not "spun" or "polished" in any way. Rather, the facts were delivered—in a way that others could see the pure, human face of the leader who was delivering the message. No invisible fence existed with Rob.

The organization ultimately decided to move its operations to Europe. And, unfortunately, there was no president position available for Rob in the end. His position was eliminated from this organization, and he went on to lead in a different setting. However, the impact that Rob left on over 1,000 employees during a difficult time was amazing. He put himself out there, was transparent and vulnerable, and, as a result, was really a role model for authenticity. Interestingly, the business results were more positive than at any time in history. In a very difficult time for people and for business, authentic leadership created an amazing response.

Taking It Personally

Although this is a business leadership example, it was also extremely personal for Rob. Rob didn't like his situation at all. But, he made a decision that revealing everything he could as a leader would be the only real way that others would be able to trust him to lead effectively during a difficult situation.

How about you? Do you struggle with accepting all of you—
even the parts you don't really like?

Do you believe that others see, know, and accept the "real" you—the one who is a blend of positive characteristics along with all your human flaws? Do you spend the majority of your life trying to be better, stronger, happier, smarter, better looking—*just more acceptable*—than you *really* believe you are? If you believe that you should improve in a certain area—and who doesn't need to do this?—which improvements are you focused most upon? Are you focused upon changing your thinking, your emotions, your heart—or are you focused only on how you can *act* differently so that you and others will see you in a certain (more acceptable) way? Are there unresolved issues from your past that have caused you to erect this invisible fence? If so, can you honestly say that you have done your part to resolve those differences?

Are you truly authentic—or are you truly just acting? We established earlier that it is what people *do* that creates personal credibility. Here's the kicker to that: What you *do* needs to line up with what you really believe—if it doesn't, then others' built-in antennae will go on alert, their HIFA alarms will sound, and trust will be difficult to establish.

Without trust, and the ability to inspire others to trust in us,
personal credibility is nearly impossible.

How about you and your invisible fence? Is there something impacting how transparent and open you are—and how others perceive you? Are you even aware of it? Try completing this simple assessment and you might be surprised.

Your response scale:

1 = Never

2 = On occasion

3 = Usually

4 = Always

1. ___ People seek me out to discuss their concerns and problems.

2. ___ I am comfortable with who I am in all areas of my life (job, family, friends, and so on).

3. ___ People value and accept me as I am.

4. ___ I have several people with whom I can easily and openly share my concerns.

5. ___ If people were asked to describe me, their descriptions would all be similar.

6. ___ I would likely agree with descriptions others have of me, my personality, and my behavior.

7. ___ I have been told that I am a good listener.

8. ___ It is very common to have total strangers approach me, begin conversations, or ask questions of me.

9. ___ When I discuss my life with others, my conversation is focused more on sharing my joys and opportunities than my problems and challenges.

10. ___ After meeting someone new, I reflect back on what I found interesting about that person.

Directions:

Add your total score: _____

Transparency Score Indicator:

> 36–40 = I am comfortable with being open, transparent, and even vulnerable.

> 29–35 = I am usually open and transparent, but might occasionally rely upon my invisible fence.

> 25–28 = I am sending some signals that I am guarded.

> Below 25 = I am guarded—my invisible fence is almost always activated.

It is a little unrealistic to advise you to "Just deactivate the invisible fence and be more transparent and authentic!" If you are trying to be authentic and transparent and it is just an act, then that act itself blocks your authenticity. The only reason that we activate our fence is to keep ourselves protected from someone or something. Why would we find a need to protect ourselves? It's because we all have some basic insecurities. We regularly ask ourselves questions like: Am I good enough? Do I really know enough? Am I really smart enough? Oh, and yes, do I look good enough? And, based on how we *really* feel about that, the fence becomes more or less a part of who we are.

Some of us are fortunate enough to know that we are neither wonderful nor terrible. We are human—each of us filled with self-belief and behaviors that run the gamut from glorious to god-awful! We eventually recognize the only way to experience effective relationships is to deactivate the invisible fence and allow others to see the real person that we are. We finally accept our own positive traits—along with our human failures and warts. If unresolved conflict from the past is creating the fence, we make a sincere effort to resolve the conflict. We commit to working on our warts, and we don't ignore them or run from the fact that they exist. When we do this, we are naturally more transparent, and we are able to experience relationships that are genuine and authentic. From doing this, we begin to trust ourselves, trust others, and gain others' trust and respect. What are we doing? We are building personal credibility.

Think about your own personal invisible fence. Does it usually stay in the "off" position, or is it almost always activated? Take a brave step and ask others for their insight. Take a look at the stress in your life and ask yourself how much might be created from the energy needed to keep that invisible fence running.

The truth about Secret #2 is this:
The easier it is for others to see the real you,
the higher your authenticity.

When others know you and believe you are authentic, you are more likely to build trust. And, when you inspire others to believe and have trust in you, you are building personal credibility.

A Final Word of Encouragement

As stated previously, it really is what we *do* that builds our personal credibility. The topic of being transparent and authentic is a little more conceptual versus practical than other topics covered in this book. Even if you found parts of this chapter somewhat difficult to translate into personal actions for building personal credibility, don't be overly concerned or discouraged. You will clearly see *how* to step up with credibility as you read more.

chapter three

Secret #3:
The Decision to Suspend Judgment

Highly credible people have made decisions to "suspend judgment"—to take a neutral position—while considering the other person's perspective. They can do this because they have decided to be OK with being wrong—or, at bare minimum, OK with having opinions challenged. People with high personal credibility are able to roll things over in their minds, consider differing perspectives, *and* stay neutral in their own positions while they do this. They have chosen neutrality as a first course. This doesn't mean they don't have passion, strong beliefs, and opinions. It simply means that their minds are able to *suspend*, to go "on hold" and be open to other opinions, ideas, and thoughts—even if those are quite different from their own!

A Frustrating Situation for Dad

"Ron" has had a tough day at work. That evening, while trying to relax and watch the evening news on TV, Ron's 10-year-old daughter, "Sarah," runs into the room and says, "Dad! My friend Molly just called and told me the National Cheerleading championship is on channel 332. Can I watch the finals?" Ron's immediate response is, "Sarah, I'm watching the news right now. No, I won't change the channel!" Sarah stares at Ron, tears bubble in her eyes, and she storms out of the room. Ron thinks about the interaction for about a minute, and then calls Sarah back in the room and says, "OK—go on and watch what you want. You can watch for 10 minutes, but that's it!" Sarah says, "Never mind, Dad, you made me miss the best part already!" She storms out again—and Ron, in frustration, thinks, "That's what I get for trying!" Ron's wife, "Susan," hears the entire episode. She says to Ron, "Why didn't you allow her to watch when she first asked? All you did was demonstrate to her that if she throws a tantrum, she might get what she wants!" Ron is getting really frustrated now. "I worked hard today to provide for this family! It should not be such a big deal to be able to come home and watch the news!" Susan now leaves in a huff! What is the problem here? Ron was not able to *suspend judgment* when his daughter made a request. There are understandable and legitimate reasons why this occurred, but the end result was damage to his personal credibility factor—with both his wife and his daughter.

Suspending judgment comes more naturally
for some than for others.

Individuals who are very decisive and take-charge types will usually struggle more with this than individuals who analyze first, and then speak. So, suspending judgment must be a *decision* we make—not just an instinct we follow. The example with Ron and his daughter probably sounds extremely familiar to most parents. But, parenting is just one arena where this secret plays out in our lives.

Hold Your Thoughts...Just for a While

"Hayley" is a bright, ambitious, young analyst in a human resources department with a fast-paced organization. The organization is growing rapidly, expanding primarily through acquiring smaller organizations in the same industry. "Sandra" is the VP of Human Resources of this organization and is facing the task of trying to consolidate all of the various employee benefit programs from the acquired organizations into one companywide program that will work for everyone. Sandra decides to work with employee benefit consultants to help her determine the best approach for structuring benefits that will be effective and acceptable to the geographically dispersed organization. The consultants have been invited to present their recommendations first to the members of the human resources department, then based on their feedback and review, they will make recommendations to senior management.

During this presentation meeting, Hayley interrupts the consultants frequently. She openly opposes their recommendations, hardly allowing the presenters to complete a sentence without interruption and challenge. Sandra decides to call a break in the meeting and brings Hayley into her office. Sandra says, "Hayley, I'm concerned that you are so quick to challenge and disagree with the consultants on their recommendations. Can you help me understand what's going on?" Hayley, clearly surprised, responds, "Sandra, I thought that is what you wanted us to do. These consultants don't know our workforce and their needs. We do. I thought you would want me to surface issues that I see as a concern!" Sandra's responds with, "Hayley, I really do want you to voice your concerns. However, I need to ask you to hold off on forming an opinion and voicing it until you have heard the entire proposal. Keep notes of your concerns. Then, let's discuss them after we've seen the big-picture proposal." Hayley stares at Sandra for a few seconds. Then, she mutters, "Well, OK," and returns to the meeting room. The meeting progressed from there, concerns and issues were discussed at the right times, and a slightly altered plan was agreed upon for presentation to senior management.

The following day, Hayley asked for a few minutes to speak with Sandra. During this discussion, she stated that she realized that she was being somewhat narrow-minded with the consultants' presentation the previous day. She also told Sandra that she had thought about that incident quite a lot. She said, "Your request for me to hold off forming an opinion (suspending judgment) until I had more information really made me think. I am pretty sure that I fail to do that regularly. It might be why I find myself getting into so many debates with people—my mind is racing forward with my own thoughts, and I am not considering the full picture while I'm doing that!"

The great news is Hayley had someone who was able to give her some coaching on a major issue regarding personal credibility when she really needed it. And, Hayley was open-minded enough to allow that lesson to affect her behavior!

Thinking Through Your Tendencies

So, why did Ron or Hayley fail to automatically suspend judgment? There are many reasons, and as stated earlier, much is connected to basic personality and communication styles. But, both are capable of making the decision to do it. Making that decision, though, requires becoming aware of what happens when we don't do it—and seeing positive value when we do!

Try this simple true/false assessment:

1. ____ When I see a need for something, I feel a strong urge to act quickly.

2. ____ When planning to eat out in a restaurant, I consider one or two options, and then quickly decide on one.

3. ____ When making a purchase decision for a different automobile, I would likely review all the makes, models, option packages, and consumer information on vehicles before looking at or driving the vehicle.

4. ____ I am irritated when someone needs a great deal of information to make a simple decision.

5. ____ I tend to stop and consider any question that is asked of me before responding with my answer.

6. ____ My automatic response to requests of me is, "Let me think about it and let you know."

If you answered "true" to statements 1, 2, or 4, it might be more difficult for you to suspend judgment. If you answered "true" to statements 3, 5, and 6, suspending judgment might be a more natural part of how you are wired as a human. There's more to it than just this one piece. Know this: If you have the instinct to act first and think second, your decision to suspend judgment will take a little more work on your part. But, the good news is this—you can choose to do it!

---

*Why does this ability to suspend judgment
have such an impact?*

It's pretty simple—when you do it, you are remaining open to all the possibilities or options within a situation. When you remain open, you are most likely to make a better decision. And, when you make the better decision in the immediate situation, you are less likely to rethink your decision, change your mind, and leave an impression on others that you are reacting to their response versus giving your own considered response.

The Thought Process for Suspending Judgment

Suspending judgment requires you to ask yourself the following questions:

- What should I learn about this situation?
- Why is it important that I remain open-minded in this situation?
- How can I respond to keep the dialogue open for more information?

So, let's look at Ron and his daughter Sarah. Here's how the conversation could play out if Ron asked himself those three questions:

That evening, while trying to relax and watch the evening news on TV, Ron's 10-year-old daughter, Sarah, runs into the room and says, "Dad! My friend Molly just called and told me the National Cheerleading championship is on channel 332. Can I see the finals?"

- Ron asks himself, *"What should I learn about this situation?"*
  Ron's first response to Sarah is now, "How much time do you need to watch this?" Sarah says, "It's in the final five minutes! I want to see who wins!"

- Ron's quick question to himself is, *"Why is this important?"* And his quick (this takes less than a second) internal response is, "Because my daughter matters to me and I love her! What's five minutes of the news when it will be repeated four times tonight anyway?"

- So, Ron now asks himself, *"How can I respond to keep the dialogue open for more information?"*
Ron's next (verbal) statement to Sarah is this, "Sure, it's fine to change the channel for five minutes if you will commit to me that you will be agreeable when I decide to change the channel back to the news that I want to watch." Sarah says, "Oh, I will, Dad!"

The channel is changed, and maybe it all works out without a hitch. Or, as often happens, perhaps Sarah wants more time to watch her preferred channel. If Ron chooses to give it to her—fine. But even if he doesn't, his credibility is still intact. Why is that? It is because he chose to suspend judgment, make a decision, and keep the communication going. She might still rant and rave, but that is not as likely now. And, remember Susan, Ron's wife? Well, she's much more likely to be pleased with Ron's response to their daughter and especially his clarifying the conditions and staying the course.

In looking at the example of Hayley, Sandra was trying to coach Hayley, and she also wanted to utilize Hayley's knowledge of the organization and employee benefits. Sandra could see that Hayley was behaving in a way that was somewhat rude and interruptive.

Appropriately, Sandra chose to address Hayley in a private conversation and used this process:

- *What should I learn about this situation?*
Sandra asked Hayley to explain why she was interrupting and not allowing the flow of the information.

- *Why is it important that I remain open-minded in this situation?*

  Sandra knew that it was important to have a trial run of the consultants' proposals to anticipate reactions from senior managers. It was important, also, to give the human resources staff the first opportunity to give feedback. Lastly, it was important that Sandra help Hayley maintain self-confidence and self-esteem, but also learn to be able to suspend judgment.

- *How can I respond to keep the dialogue open for more information?*

  Sandra responded to Hayley in private, to protect her from public criticism. She also asked questions versus just giving direction. And, she responded by giving an alternative way for Hayley to handle the situation by choosing to suspend judgment. Lastly, she made it clear that she wanted Hayley's thoughts and questions—she just wanted her to present those in a different manner. Today, Hayley claims that this became a major moment of learning for her.

Suspending judgment is an action that takes just a very small amount of time.

Typically, this thought process occurs in one to three seconds, believe it or not. However, when we use those few seconds and practice the process, we have an incredible opportunity to increase personal credibility. We avoid hasty decisions. We postpone our own reactions that could harm relationships. We are far less likely to face a situation of changing our mind and our position on issues as a result. Others learn to trust us to think/then act, rather than act/then change our mind. When others can depend on us to do that, we are seen as someone who is believable and trustworthy—someone with personal credibility.

For Personal Credibility: Know the Secrets!

As we learned in Part I, people who possess strong personal credibility tend to share an understanding of these simple secrets:

- Respect is earned from what we do, not from position, status, or power.

- Trust only happens when people know that we are sincere and transparent.

- We greatly increase our chances for earning trust and respect when we choose to suspend judgment of others—and keep our minds open to considering other perspectives.

So, it always ties back to one central point: When we give and receive trust and respect, we are on the road to personal credibility!

Part II

Stepping Up with Credibility: Seven Steps to Influence Personal Credibility

Perhaps you thought as you have been reading, "Well, Alice clearly had more *influence* than John," or "Mitch's *influence* on others was more positive than Chuck's." You might also have registered the thought that Pete *lost* influence with others when he was critical behind the backs of the same people whose ego he stroked. And, the reality is that this is true—personal credibility is definitely impacted by an individual's ability to influence others. Over time, positive influence creates greater credibility, negative influence reduces it. There is really no question about it.

Understanding Influence and Personal Credibility

Effective leaders—and this includes leading within a workplace, leading within our own families, or simply leading a productive individual life—are in a position to have influence on others. As you read in Secret #2, "I Can See Right Through You," credibility is not established as a result of the power or authority of the position someone holds. Credible results are, instead, based upon the individual's ability to behave in a way that creates positive responses from others. It doesn't really matter what relationship we are discussing—friends, family, churches, or any business or organization. Leaders who are effective over the long term are able to positively influence followers. Effective leaders, through positive influence, create the *desire* in others to follow, learn, and emulate positive behaviors.

In Part II, you review specific behaviors and actions you can take to increase your ability to positively influence others and enhance your own personal credibility as a result. The word influence simply means to *sway the thoughts and opinions* of others. The reality is that we all have influence that we apply daily—it's just a question of whether we're realizing positive, neutral, or negative results.

To be clear, not all influence is positive—for example, parents of teenagers can readily understand the concern that occurs when their teens begin spending time with friends who are involved in activities that are not healthy and potentially dangerous. The concern is that the values and behaviors of their sons and daughters will be adversely impacted—negatively influenced—by the bad choices and habits of their peers. Teen peers have a great deal of opportunity to sway the thoughts and opinions of their friends. Teens are swayed by influencers—and that can have a very detrimental impact!

> *The good news is that healthy, positive influencers also leave a lasting impact.*

When you consider the word *influence*, what immediately comes to your mind? Is it always a totally positive term? Do you think of the word *sales*? Unless you have had the opportunity to be educated and trained in professional selling skills, the terms influence and sales might conjure thoughts of being pushed or forced in a direction that isn't comfortable for you. Or, perhaps you think of a fast-talking, slick sales type who is trying to sell you something you don't want or need. For now, try to "suspend judgment" on any thoughts you might have that influence is really about smooth talking or slick image. Don't even think of it as someone who is very gifted at persuading others. Instead, read further and learn more about the regular, daily types of actions that create lasting positive influence and build your personal credibility factor. Explore the following straight-forward but proven methods that create real influence and drive our personal credibility factors forward:

- **Step #1**—Know Your "Stuff"
- **Step #2**—Keep Commitments
- **Step #3**—Honor Confidences and Avoid Gossip
- **Step #4**—Know Yourself—the Good, the Bad, and the Ugly!
- **Step #5**—Choose to Value Others—the Good, and Yes, Even the Bad and the Ugly!
- **Step #6**—Ask More and Listen Most
- **Step #7**—Create Credible Interactions

chapter four

Step #1:
Know Your "Stuff"

You've likely heard or even made this comment about someone: "_____ really knows her stuff!" What do we really mean when we make that statement? Usually, it means that someone has positively impressed us with their knowledge and, likely, their ability to apply that knowledge. "Knowing your stuff" means becoming knowledgeable, skilled, and making a commitment to doing your best in whatever you do. When you know your stuff, it is so much easier to be authentic because you are confident in what you know and do.

Parents are more credible when they have educated themselves on the value of making thoughtful decisions about raising kids, and then applying a consistent approach to raising those kids. Physicians are more credible when they continue to seek knowledge and information on advancements in medical practices and are able to help patients take advantage of the most current and valid information. A friend is more credible when he/she understands what a friend is in need of, and consciously seeks to provide that for the friend. An employee who makes a decision to increase knowledge or capability of doing the job becomes more credible—and more likely to be considered for future promotional opportunities.

The bottom line is this: Credibility begins with doing whatever we do regularly with a strong commitment to becoming the best "whatever" we can be for that time, place, and situation.

Learning As She Goes

Remember "Sandra"? She was the VP of Human Resources who helped "Hayley" understand the value of suspending judgment. Sandra has a story, too. Earlier in her life, Sandra spent several years learning the ropes in the human resource management profession. She was in a tough spot in the early years—having been divorced at 24-years-old and the mother of two-year-old twins. She struggled financially— trying to do everything humanly possible to support her young family. While performing primarily administrative duties on her job, she was given several opportunities to volunteer on some important higher-level work projects. She believed working on these projects could provide her an opportunity to learn more, possibly expand her role, and become more valuable to the organization. Her problem? She knew very little about the project topics or how to do the work! Her only option was to read, study, ask questions of those more experienced, and put hard work into those projects to create successes. So, Sandra read manuals and books at night, studied during lunch breaks, and generally consumed information about the topic of the projects she worked on. She worked like a wild woman! Because she saw her only option as working hard and learning the ropes, Sandra was given many opportunities to continue progressing—and continue learning.

What did Sandra really learn through this process? She learned to consider it a requirement of the current job to learn what to do and how to do it. She admits that she had a distant hope that her career would progress, but she didn't expect it. She did it for the "here and now"—to be of value today—for today's work. She worked because she was being given an opportunity to work hard and perform. She really didn't focus on what might come of it other than the chance to earn another paycheck and demonstrate that she was a good employee. People with strong personal credibility tend to believe that they are responsible for becoming more and more knowledgeable. They assume that they do not know it all—and they assume responsibility for increasing their own knowledge. Sandra had no idea when she was a struggling, young, single mom that she was building her personal credibility factor by making sure that she knew her stuff! But, she is very thankful now that she chose to assume responsibility, learn more, and work hard!

How Do I Make Sure That I Know My Stuff?

Most of us can agree that people are more credible when they clearly demonstrate knowledge and a willingness to continually learn. Sandra chose to pursue knowledge and continue to become more valuable to her employer. She also chose to sacrifice her free time in order to accomplish this, even though she had precious little free time to give. No matter where we are in life, we can choose to seek more knowledge and become more effective in whatever we are doing. Consider the following actions for increasing your own abilities to "know your stuff."

Gain an Appetite for Knowledge—Consider It Credibility Survival!

Unfortunately, we are living in a world where it is becoming much easier to just "coast." We get information fairly easily. Really, how hard is it to do an Internet search whenever we are curious about something? But, this readily available information hasn't necessarily inspired us to want to learn more—it has often caused us to take information and learning for granted! You know your stuff not just as a result of having information or knowledge, but when you are able to give examples and apply that knowledge in a way that helps accomplish something and helps others. When your appetite for knowledge and learning increases, you adopt a "What can I learn about this?" thought process.

Read!

Read books, magazines, journals, articles—anything that can help you learn and understand more so that you can provide more. Of course, no one has time to read constantly, but if you give an hour per week to reading for learning's sake, you will be amazed at how quickly you will learn, and how that reading will inspire you to do even more!

Seek Wise Counsel

Regardless of the role or situation, there are people who have more wisdom and experience than we have in that same area. If you aspire to be a mom or dad with strong personal credibility, think of other moms or dads you know who stand out in certain aspects of their roles. Seek their advice, ask for their experiences, and learn from their successes—and their mistakes!

Think of others who have succeeded and have strong personal credibility. Ask for an opportunity to talk with someone who stands out in your mind. Explain that you have made observations of how effective that individual is and how credible he or she is as a result. Ask for examples of how that person has been able to establish their credibility. Ask for the opportunity to be mentored by that individual. Most people are very willing to provide mentoring and coaching, and many are truly honored to be asked!

Know the Enemy (Its Name Is Apathy!)

Individuals who continually learn and grow add more value—and are automatically more credible as a result of that growth. Sure, it is very easy to think, "I have 20 years of experience in this area—I really don't need to learn any more!" Although it is true that your interests and areas of focus might change dramatically over the years, it is also true that ongoing learning allows you to achieve ongoing credibility. The only challenge is that this requires ongoing *work*—and we do tend to get somewhat complacent, especially when we feel like we have achieved a level of expertise in an area. Understand what apathy looks like for you personally and make a commitment to keep on knowing your stuff—even if your stuff changes over time!

Regardless of your role in life, you are more credible when you accept ownership for gaining knowledge about it and work to keep that knowledge current. If you are in the real estate profession, this means ensuring you are up to speed on real estate contracts, even if you much prefer interacting with clients and selling! If you are a hair stylist, it means staying current with styles and trends and the most current methods for achieving those. If you are a stay-at-home parent, it means keeping informed on the best ways to manage households and families, and working every day toward becoming even more effective. If you are a parent who works outside the home, you are more credible when you seek and obtain knowledge to create an effective balance between your work life and your personal life. People who are most credible don't assume that it is anyone's job but their own to gain that knowledge and keep building on it!

The reality is this: To know your stuff, you have to keep learning new stuff!

chapter five

Step #2:
Keep Commitments

Let's go back to the very frustrating yet common issue of dealing with contractors for household projects. You set up an appointment with a contractor to give you an estimate for installing a new deck on your home. One contractor might keep that appointment, but never provides the estimate. You follow up and leave a message about the estimate, but never receive a return phone call. Another contractor might not even show up for the appointment to give the estimate in the first place! Another one provides the estimate, sets up the work plan, but then doesn't show up to do the work. What on Earth is this all about? Why don't people keep these basic types of commitments?

---

*If we think about it, many of us violate this
basic principle regularly.*

We tell a friend, "Let's get together for lunch over the next couple of weeks," but never follow through to set it up. Even worse, we mention a tentative date, and then fail to finalize that date or show up. Or, how about this: We are in a very busy time of our lives. We receive a voice mail message or e-mail from a friend or coworker asking that we call to discuss something. We really mean to do that…but, somehow, we forget. Perhaps you indicate to a coworker that you will complete a project by the end of the day, and don't quite get it done. Perhaps you approach that person sometime the next day, and quickly say, "Sorry, I know this wasn't done by the end of yesterday, but here you go." This seems like no big deal, right? Maybe—but maybe not!

These are the small, daily actions that significantly impact our credibility over time. Most of us are willing to forgive an occasional slipup—but when the same people do the same sort of thing over a period of time, they lose credibility with us! We are not likely to believe or trust what they say in the future.

Commitments Break Down and Invisible Fences Go Up

Remember "Donna"? She had the impenetrable invisible fence activated in her relationship with her family. She was definitely not someone who demonstrated authenticity and transparency on that front. Donna had quite a reputation for making commitments for contributing to family dinners or gatherings, and then regularly did not come through for the event. She would commit to helping out with specific items for a wedding shower given for a family member, then inevitably show up late without bringing the items she had promised to bring.

She would commit to bringing a menu item for family gatherings—and then cancel at the last minute. Seems like a small thing, but over time, family members just knew she would likely not come through. It's likely that Donna made as many excuses to herself as she did to her family—and the result was always the same. Donna had little credibility with her family. Instead of apologizing, she would develop outlandish excuses and justifications for her lack of commitment. Unfortunately, Donna's behavior only continued to build the strength of her invisible fence. What did she need to do to fix this? It really could have begun with just keeping the commitments she made.

Keeping Small Commitments Adds Up to Big Credibility

Let's revisit "John" and "Alice" from "Secret #1: Forget Power, Position, Status, and Other Such Nonsense." John was not successful at having his great recommendations and ideas approved by the senior management group at his company. As a result of some organizational restructuring, John began reporting to Alice. Alice was quickly able to gain commitment and agreement on most of John's proposed recommendations that had been previously shot down by senior management.

When you dig into this situation, you learn that John was perceived as someone who didn't always keep commitments. But it wasn't necessarily with the big things—instead, it was the small things. John was relatively famous for failing to return voice mail messages or e-mail messages. His daily calendar was frequently filled, which didn't allow for unplanned interruptions. Because unplanned interruptions were the norm, John was faced with rescheduling meetings—sometimes two or three times before a meeting would occur. Over time, other leaders in the organization would comment cynically when John would schedule, then reschedule, meetings. When John did show up for meetings, he was always a little late and seemed harried. So—even though he had great ideas and recommendations—he also had a problem with personal credibility.

Then, Alice enters the scene. Alice is someone who is very organized, ensures that all messages are returned, and keeps her calendar filled, but also allows time for the unexpected. Alice has other personal credibility attributes going for her, but the first one that makes the most difference in getting the recommendations and ideas accepted and approved is that Alice keeps commitments—and her fellow leaders have confidence that the recommendations will now be implemented effectively.

Why did John struggle with keeping commitments, but Alice, with similar demands and responsibilities, could handle multiple commitments and competing priorities with such positive results? There are really just a few basic differences, but the difference these made are huge! If you recall, John asked Alice how she had been able to accomplish gaining approval of the same ideas and recommendations that he had previously failed to achieve. After thinking through her actions and how they contrasted to some of John's, Alice realized that there were some basic principles that she had learned from two of her former bosses. She also realized that she followed these principles regularly. She shared them with John, and he was able to readily see that he needed to focus on his methods of keeping commitments.

Commitment Difference Makers

Review the following list and consider how you might increase your focus on areas that could positively impact your delivery on commitments:

- *Avoid overcommitment*—Be realistic with yourself and others about your ability to do something. An upfront "I just can't make that commitment at this point" is so much more effective than "I'm so sorry; I just couldn't get that done."

- *Schedule daily "communication" time*—Use this time to return phone calls, e-mails, send birthday or thank-you cards, and keep current with communication. It's best to do this at about the same time daily so that it becomes a habit. Build the time into your calendar—you are building personal credibility when you do it!

- *Keep time open between appointments*—It's ridiculous to think you can move from issue to issue without time for transition and handling unexpected issues that surface.

- *One place, one record*—Whether you do this electronically or on paper, have one single place where you record messages received, notes from conversations, appointments, to-do lists, project milestones, grocery lists, doctor appointments, children's soccer games and dance recitals, and everything occurring in your life. If it is in one place, it will be much easier to see the reality of your schedule and be easier to avoid overcommitting. You also will dramatically reduce the chance of forgetting about a commitment.

- *Keep others informed if conditions change*—If something happens and you suspect you might not be able to keep a commitment, let that person know immediately. The worst thing possible is to try to ignore what is happening—instead, step up, acknowledge the changed condition, and keep everyone who will be impacted informed.

Clearly, these principles can help out in the workplace, but they can also be helpful in our personal lives. For example, "Shawna" is a busy mother of four adult children and nine grandchildren. Shawna and her husband "Ward" also have busy careers, serve in their church, and keep active social calendars. It's sometimes difficult, but they want to make sure they spend time with their children and grandchildren. Shawna is the one who usually makes the social arrangements with friends and schedules time with family members. How does she do it? She uses the same method. Here is how it works:

- *Avoid overcommitment*—Shawna and Ward know that although they want to have time with everyone, it is clear that they must also have time to recuperate and rest! So, they have established limits for their schedule. For example, they never schedule weekends that stay filled with activities from Friday to Sunday. They make sure that each weekend includes downtime for the two of them, and this usually means either Friday night or Sundays, and preferably both!

- *Schedule daily communication time*—This can be challenging, but both Shawna and Ward try to put family first and make certain that they are in adequate contact with children, grandchildren, and their aging parents on a regular basis. So, this typically means that phone calls, e-mails, birthday cards, and so on are handled early in the day before the workday begins. This might mean an earlier wake-up alarm at times, but it is their way to know they can prioritize and ensure that family does, indeed, come first. In addition, their children and parents know that they can expect early versus late contacts from Shawna and Ward, and can also plan accordingly. It works for them!

- *Keep time open between appointments*—As we can see, this is a busy couple with many irons in the fire. One thing that both Shawna and Ward have learned is that the quality of their lives is clearly linked to their ability to exercise regularly. It works best for them to do this first thing in the morning, just after waking up and drinking a cup of coffee. Because they both run their own businesses, they have flexibility in their schedules. They have learned, however, that they need to build in time between their daily workouts and the rest of the day. They allow 45 minutes for workouts, 45 minutes for daily grooming, and then 30 minutes to catch up with communications. This adds up to a two-hour time frame. However, they both allow 2.5 hours before their first appointment to allow for catching their breath and for unforeseen activities. Shawna also sets appointments with a minimum of 30 minutes between appointments to allow for catching up on e-mails or whatever issues have occurred during the day. Each allows a minimum of a 45-minute drive time for drives that typically take about 20 minutes. This allows both of them the time to stay current on any unforeseen issues and avoid dropping the ball on any unexpected issues that might come their way. It also helps them avoid unwanted stresses that will automatically occur when the schedule is too tight for reality.

- **One place, one record**—Because Shawna keeps up with the social and family schedule, both work and non–work related activities go on her calendar. She uses a daily system of keeping a log of messages received and messages returned. She integrates her business and personal to-do list into a single list and keeps it checked off, transferring any uncompleted items to the next day. She keeps Ward informed on any updates, changes, or schedule additions via e-mail.

- ***Keep others informed if conditions change***—And, they do change—these people are normal people, so, of course, conditions change. For example, Shawna's aging parents are often dependent on Shawna to take them to doctor appointments. Shawna also knows that she might need to rely on her brother or one of her children for this if she has any unexpected business issues that surface that could change her availability. The moment she sees that there might be a schedule conflict, she quickly e-mails her brother and children to see if anyone might be able to fill in for her to transport one of her parents to a doctor. If someone is readily available, she quickly gains their commitment to take care of the transportation. Note that she does not wait until she is certain there is a conflict. She knows it is better to make alternative arrangements and have herself available as a backup if needed than to wait until the last minute. Her other family members appreciate her willingness to take responsibility for coordinating all of this for her parents, and readily jump in and help when they are needed.

Perhaps you are thinking that it would be impractical to put such structure into your personal life. Yet, our personal lives usually include the ones who matter most! So, why shouldn't we do everything we can to earn the trust and respect of the ones who mean the most to us? When we are able to keep commitments with those who matter most to us, we are most likely to be trusted and valued by them.

Personal credibility is exactly that—personal!

chapter six

Step #3:
Honor Confidences and
Avoid Gossip

"Please don't tell anyone this, but..." How many conversations have you either started or been a part of that began in this way? Most of us make a quick, easy commitment to keep that confidence. And then, we tell just one person who would never repeat it anyway, right? When information is shared that was given in confidence, the "one person" we share it with might actually keep the information strictly confidential—but what does the fact that you chose to share it say about your ability to keep confidences? Yep, that's right. Your credibility is not increased from sharing information—it is actually decreased, and sometimes dramatically.

With the Best of Intentions

This is a tough area—we are human and many of us love hearing and learning information that might be a little dicey or could be someone's secret. Often, we love it so much that we might be unintentionally sacrificing friendships, working relationships, our organization's business, or just about anything else. We don't think consciously that we are destroying our own personal credibility when we break confidences or engage in gossip, but, indeed, we are. We have the option of totally controlling this aspect of personal credibility and can reap significant benefits by simply making a strong commitment here. Let's take a look at a simple example of how this issue can impact our personal credibility.

You have a group of friends who have shared good times and activities together for several years. At a recent dinner gathering of the group, "Sam" and "Jim" were involved in a disagreement that became somewhat heated. Feelings have been damaged a little as a result. Both Sam and Jim individually contact you to seek your advice on how to handle the disagreement. You give both your advice, agree to keep your discussions confidential, and hope that by taking your advice they will work it out and retain their friendship.

Then, another friend, "Chris," contacts you and shares with you that Sam and Jim have also contacted him confidentially and asked for his advice, and then proceeds to tell you how he has advised them to work this out. His advice is identical to your advice, so you say, "Please don't share this with anyone, but…." You let him know that both of you have provided the same advice, and you end the conversation when you both express a sincere desire for these two to work it out, heed your mutual advice, and resolve the conflict.

Your interest is in the relationship being repaired with these two friends, so how could you lose credibility? The moment you say, "Please don't tell anyone, but..." credibility begins to erode. Perhaps none of this will ever get back to the two people to whom you committed confidentiality. But, what message are you sending to Chris about your ability to manage confidences? You might be thinking Chris also has a credibility issue because he shared confidential information with you. This is true, but the only person in this whole situation that you can control is yourself. Your appropriate response should have been, "I care about these two friends of ours as well. I'm just not sure we should be discussing anything about them that we aren't discussing directly with them." And, at the very least, you could have—and should have—just kept your commitment of confidentiality about your conversation. If information is shared with you, you could listen, express your hope that these two work it out, and then move on to another topic.

This might seem somewhat trivial. The reality is this:
People who have a high personal credibility factor are
people who keep confidences and find ways to avoid
becoming involved in gossip.

Here are some simple tips for handling daily situations that might impact your personal credibility factor in this area. Remember this:

- You have high personal credibility when you are someone who can be trusted. Even the perception of breaking confidences can destroy the trust, thus your credibility.

- When you are unsure if you are actually engaging in gossip, ask yourself, "If this person whom I'm talking about appears at this moment, would the conversation change at all?" If the answer is yes, don't discuss it.

- If you have been guilty of breaking confidences or engaging in gossip previously, make a commitment to change. Just simply say, "I'm sure I don't know all the facts," and then change the subject. Not only will you leave the impression that you won't share confidences and participate in gossip, you will cause the other person who is trying to engage you to stop and think about his or her own actions.

The Truth Behind the Gossip

The truth about this topic is sometimes difficult to face. We often share information or participate in gossip because doing so appears to give us more power or boost our own self-esteem. We feel a little more powerful when we have information that others don't have. We feel a little more important when others will share information with us that might not be known or readily available to others. Or, we might even think others will like and respect us more if we show them that we trust them with information that is confidential.

Most of us want to "fit in" with others, and sometimes the sharing of confidential information gives us the sense that we are fitting in very well—that we are in the "club" or inside circle within a group. Ultimately, respect erodes when others learn that we can't be trusted with sensitive information.

At some point, we really need to make a decision:
Are we seeking short-term acceptance or
long-term respect and trust?

It's the long-term approach toward respect and trust when handling confidential information and avoiding gossip that will earn personal credibility.

chapter seven

Step #4:
Know Yourself—the Good,
the Bad, and the Ugly!

Individuals with strong personal credibility typically have a high level of self-awareness. They are usually very aware of their own strengths, as well as their own weaknesses. They know themselves accurately and typically have an ability to see both their strengths and weaknesses in a factual, objective manner. They tend to constantly keep that awareness in mind when interacting with others.

She Knew Herself and Understood

If you recall, "Alice" was able to gain approval from the senior leaders of the organization for most of "John's" previous recommendations. One of the reasons Alice was so successful in this area was that she was extremely aware of her own style of communication and preferences, and was able to adjust or flex her style as she worked with others. Alice knew that she personally preferred to see and analyze a great deal of data that would support a new business idea before making final decisions. She also knew that many of her peers on the leadership team had this same preference. John was more of a "seat-of-the-pants" type. He could conceive great "big-picture" possibilities and expected others to be able to see those ideas in the same way he did. John wanted others to share his enthusiasm for the idea, but he was not inclined to spend the time building the case with data to support his idea. Alice was able to work with John, develop the data that she and many of the other leaders needed to see, and then help John move his terrific new ideas forward.

Alice also knew that she had a tendency to get mired in analyzing the details of an idea, which could cause ideas to stall out and not be implemented. An idea or recommendation could totally lose momentum while she and her staff worked on gathering the details to support it. As a result of her self-awareness, she purposefully chose to surround herself with people who could do two things: Think outside the box— be very open to new and untried ideas—and give her direct feedback when she was causing the idea to lose momentum as a result of her data-gathering tendencies. The key here is that she was self-aware enough to know her own tendencies, and developed successful strategies to help her overcome those that might impede her success. As a result, she increased personal credibility. Others naturally respected and valued her as a result of her very objective self-awareness.

Third Time Is the Charm

"Roy" is a loving and compassionate husband. He is committed to his marriage, and his wife knows that she is the highest priority in his life. Roy is also a very outspoken man. He speaks his thoughts as he is thinking them—his wife often says that he thinks with his mouth! Roy had two prior marriages before his current marriage. After much counseling and self-assessment, Roy realized that his tendency to speak first, and then think about the impact of his words had caused a great deal of negative impact on his prior marriages. So, when he met and fell in love with his current wife of 26 years, he did a smart thing. He told her about his past failed marriages and his own communication tendencies. He also made it clear that he needed to be in a relationship with someone who could both accept the way his brain and mouth worked—yet at the same time be strong enough to let him know when his tendencies were having a negative impact. He promised an open mind and a sincere desire to learn a different approach. He has not failed to deliver on his promise. The marriage works beautifully for many reasons, not the least of which is that Roy finally learned his good, his bad, and his ugly!

Do you see that both Alice and John brought definite strengths to the organization? Whereas John spent quite a lot of energy trying to convince the other leaders of the organization to think like him, Alice recognized that both big-picture thinking and the ability to provide supporting details were critical. She knew very well what her tendencies were—and she knew that she needed to keep others around her who were capable of thinking differently.

Roy has so much to offer in a marriage relationship. His married life became successful when he realized his own tendencies, openly shared what he knew about himself, and made the commitment to remain open to adjusting his communication methods when they created a negative impact. In his wife's eyes, Roy is someone with very strong personal credibility.

People with strong personal credibility tend to have a high level of self-awareness.

Self-awareness naturally extends to having "others-awareness." Individuals who have thought about their own personality and communication styles usually understand that all styles or tendencies bring both strengths and challenges. They are naturally more accepting of others because they tend to avoid thinking in terms of right and wrong, good or bad—but instead think in terms of *differences* in style and communications.

There are many style or preference indicators available to help you determine your own style. Tools such as the Myers-Briggs Type Indicator, the DISC personality profile, or the Insight Inventory are just a few. Most are easy to complete and can be helpful to gain increased self-awareness. If you have not had the opportunity to complete one of these, you might want to consider doing that. Using any computer search engine, simply search "Personal Communication Styles" to learn more about various instruments and how you can access them. Many are free of charge.

The following overview might help you in considering your personal tendencies and increase self-awareness:

Please check one statement that is *more like you* in each section below. (This is a forced response process. Understand that neither statement might reflect your exact style. You should choose the one that is an indication of your stronger tendencies.)

Section 1: Ideas or Evidence?

a. ___ I prefer to think about the big picture, possible ideas, or new concepts that might be possible.

b. ___ I prefer to have significant supporting information and data before I form a conclusion or make a decision about something.

Section 2: Direct or Diplomatic?

a. ___ I say what I am thinking, sometimes coming across in a blunt manner.

b. ___ I carefully choose words so that I won't create conflict or damage feelings.

Section 3: Retreat or Engage?

a. ___ I know that I need time alone to allow me to restore my energy if I am tired.

b. ___ Even when I'm tired, I will quickly become energized when I am with other people.

Section 4: Options or Plans?

a. ___ I like to keep all my options open before committing to a plan of action.

b. ___ I am uncomfortable in a situation where it seems there is no clear plan for what will occur.

What does this tell you?

Section 1: Ideas or Evidence?

Ideas

If you checked (a), you are a big-picture thinker and can see many options and ideas. You avoid becoming overly consumed in the details, which helps both you and others keep the focus on the ultimate goals or opportunities.

Watch Out *for falling into the same situation as John. Understand that you will need to provide more data or detail to meet the needs of others, and if you are unwilling or unable to provide that detail, you might need to find alternative ways to gather it.*

Evidence

If you checked (b), you have a desire for more precision and information. You automatically find ways to gather and assimilate data to support decisions, and want to be sure that the facts have been carefully reviewed and considered before final conclusions are developed. To you, trying new things without any evidence of their potential success doesn't make a lot of sense.

Watch Out *for paralysis by analysis. There are many times when less is more—accept the fact that more information is sometimes just duplication of the same data. Be careful that you don't squelch the fire and energy behind others' ideas by slowing down the decision-making process too long.*

Section 2: Direct or Diplomatic?

Direct

If you checked (a), you are very direct in your communications. You do not hesitate to give your thoughts and openly address any differences of opinions with others when they surface. There is rarely any hidden agenda or unaddressed conflict with you. Others clearly know where you stand.

Watch Out *for others' misunderstanding your directness as rudeness. Although you might believe you are simply presenting an opinion or giving clear direction, others might view you as being dictatorial and closed to any other perspective.*

Diplomatic

If you checked (b), you prefer a more thoughtful, diplomatic approach of communicating. You are sensitive to conflict, and want to choose words and language that will lessen the chance for conflict or damaged feelings.

Watch Out *for being unclear. In your desire to be diplomatic, you could be perceived as being wishy-washy or having no clear position on an issue. If you are directing others' actions, they might conclude that you are making suggestions versus giving direction.*

Section 3: Retreat or Engage?

Retreat

If you checked (a), you are energized by having time to think and reflect. You prefer winding down at the end of the day by being alone or with very few people. You are willing to allow others to take center stage and find it difficult to interrupt or interject when someone else is speaking. You tend to listen carefully to what others say and provide thoughtful reflection on their thoughts.

Watch Out *for being overlooked. In your desire to give others the floor to speak, you can easily miss opportunities to express your thoughts and ideas, even when they are really valuable and needed. Your quiet respect for others might cause them to believe that you have little to offer.*

Engage

If you checked (b), you are energized by being with other people, and enjoy talking and expressing yourself. Because you are energized by others, you tend to give energy back to them. Groups will often become livelier when you are in the picture. It makes you uncomfortable when it appears others are not engaged, and you tend to feel responsible for engaging them.

Watch Out *for overwhelming people. You might be perceived as being someone who needs all the attention, especially when you do not use effective listening skills. Understand that people express comfort in different ways, and that it is not your job to energize the world. Be sure to ask people their thoughts and ideas, not just give yours.*

Section 4: Options or Plans?

Options

If you checked (a), you realize there are several ways to accomplish something, and you have the opportunity to change your mind as you go. You enjoy responding spontaneously, and feel overly restrained when your plans become too rigid. You are often the person who suggests trying out new things.

Watch Out *for starting things that you don't finish. Because you respond spontaneously, you might find it difficult to focus on issues long enough to complete them. When you fail to complete things, including the commitments that you make, others might lose trust in your ability to follow through.*

Plans

If you checked (b), you understand that results require the development of plans, and you are always thinking two or three steps ahead. You are usually well prepared, and become somewhat frustrated when others don't develop or follow plans. After you have put a structure in place for anything, you are more confident and relaxed.

Watch Out *for being too rigid and stressing out when changes occur. In your desire to put a plan in place for everything, you might miss out on experiencing the beauty or magic of the moment. It's helpful to be prepared, but not if it causes you to miss out on what you were planning for all along because you were too busy thinking about the next step.*

STEP #4: KNOW YOURSELF—THE GOOD, THE BAD, AND THE UGLY!

There are many aspects of becoming self-aware. Awareness of our own communication styles and tendencies will help us to understand how we tick. As a result, we can maximize our positive aspects, while also managing the "watch outs"—which can occasionally get a little ugly! Personal credibility is about being authentic and real—but also about having enough self-awareness to understand that your tendencies and preferences might be different from others with whom you are interacting. Individuals who possess strong personal credibility begin by understanding themselves so that they can then better understand and interact with others.

chapter eight

Step #5:
Choose to Value Others—
the Good, and Yes, Even the Bad
and the Ugly!

In the last chapter, we discussed how self-awareness of personal style and preferences of communication impacts personal credibility. When we are able to take an *objective* view of our own communication tendencies and styles, we can assess how our style might work well with some people, and probably not so well with others.

There is a natural connection between self-awareness and increasing our awareness, and sensitivity to, others' tendencies and styles.

Individuals who possess strong personal credibility tend to assess others from a more objective perspective because they are more objective about their own strengths and style issues. When we are objective, we avoid thinking of others in terms of "good" or "bad" or "right" or "wrong." Instead, we think in terms of our styles of communication—both in how we are similar or different from those around us.

Ideas or Evidence?

If you recall, "John" was definitely a big-picture thinker. He had great *ideas* and incredible creative energy. He could think of various possible solutions to problems and challenges and enjoyed any opportunity to present and discuss his thoughts and ideas. John worked with several other leaders whose styles differed. Some tended to be suspicious of any idea that did not have factual evidence and proof to support it. "David" was one of those other leaders who wanted to see the *evidence* (facts and data) to support any idea. David and John had frequent clashes. Their disagreements became somewhat predictable whenever John presented recommendations for the organization's consideration. John said, "I think this could be a great strategy..." and David quickly responded, "Don't take our time with great ideas unless you have some facts to support it, John." John's usual response was to be critical of David's resistance to change, and then David would criticize John's willingness to waste time and organizational resources. The clash often turned into a war of words, with nothing accomplished except increasingly damaged relationships.

David and John were both part of the organization's pilot executive development program. One part of this program focused on raising awareness of various communication styles and how these styles can either create conflict or incredible value, depending upon how people handled their differing styles. Another senior leader in attendance, "Mary Ann," approached both John and David individually. She asked each, "Do you think it's possible that your style differences could be causing the conflicts between you?" Both spent some time thinking about it, and later, each initiated follow-up conversations with Mary Ann. Both David and John came to the realization that the major cause for their conflict was indeed differences in style. Mary Ann was exactly right. But what could solve the issue? Neither could change the person that he was—nor did he have any desire to do so. Eventually, Mary Ann volunteered to "facilitate" a conversation between David and John. She brought them together and asked the following questions of each:

- How could each of you benefit from communicating more effectively?
- What could the other person say or do differently that could help this to occur?
- What could you say or do differently that might help?
- What are you going to do to make that happen?

The end result of this conversation was amazing. In this neutral, objective environment, both David and John became much more aware of his own tendencies. Each was able to give specific ideas about what could be done to improve the situation from his perspective. Most important, each decided to value the other person. Each made commitments to attempt to "flex" his style for better communications to occur. And both did it.

Both John and David made agreements to consider the other's style going forward. John, the *ideas* person, made adjustments to his style in the following way:

- He "labeled" his discussion topics more. If he wanted the group to brainstorm ideas, he told them that. If he was presenting various options that could be considered in the future, he told them that. If he was presenting one idea that he wanted to get a decision made about, he made that clear. This allowed David and the others to hear John out in the appropriate context—without jumping to conclusions and stopping the development of ideas.

- He summarized his ideas first. No long, drawn-out discussion of any idea occurred without John's first laying out his ideas in a very brief form.

- When he was making a recommendation for the group's approval, he gathered more data to support his ideas and recommendations and only recommended those ideas that were supported with facts and data.

- He prioritized his recommendations based on which would have the most positive, organizational impact.

- He learned to present all the positives and possible downsides to an idea—and he informed people in advance that he was prepared to do that.

David, the *evidence* person, also made some adjustments to his style and preferences:

- He suspended judgment until he had fully heard John's ideas.

- He learned to brainstorm—to participate in a process of getting all the ideas to surface before attempting to narrow them down and look for evidence to support them.

- Instead of attacking the person or the issue, he simply asked the question, "Do you have any evidence or data to support this idea?" When he felt that evidence was lacking, he learned to ask, "When are you going to develop this data?"

- He also adjusted his own style when he presented to others. He learned to tell people what to expect—to "label" his own presentations as well. He often said, "I have the final recommendations. I have the details to support all of these recommendations. I'll present the major recommendations first, and then feel free to ask me about any data that I've gathered that will support each recommendation." This reflected a big change for David as well. He had frequently presented every detail up front, boring half his audience—mostly because he assumed everyone wanted that level of data and support for ideas, just as he did. When he became more aware of differences, he used this to help him not only with John, but with his presentations and discussions with the entire leadership team. Many were very relieved!

The choice to "value others" in the preceding example occurred when each person considered how having better communications could benefit both parties. They were both fortunate to have the benefit of Mary Ann, who was able to objectively assess their conflict and take the initiative to discuss it with them. The focus was then able to move away from who was right or who was wrong—and moved toward working more effectively together.

It can be very difficult to value others. Some "others" are downright difficult people! A few are nasty, mean-spirited, and truly seem to enjoy hurting or harming others. But most are just people—with different styles of communication. When we choose first to value that person, we open the door to problem solving and a productive relationship success.

With successful relationships, respect occurs. Respect, given and received, creates personal credibility.

What about you? Are you struggling in a relationship that might be based upon a difference in styles? Is it possible that one of those differences is in this area of ***ideas or evidence***? You? can allow Mary Ann's questions for John and David to help you as well. Think through this relationship, consider your own personal preference and the other individual's likely preference, and then respond to these questions:

- How could each of you benefit from communicating more effectively?

  _____

  _____

  _____

- What could the other person say or do differently that could help this to occur?

  _____

  _____

  _____

- What could you say or do differently that might help?

  _____

  _____

  _____

- What are you going to do to make that happen?

  _____

  _____

  _____

You have likely had experiences when it is difficult to value someone else. Ask yourself: Is it the *person* that I struggle with finding the value with, or is it the difference in style that is getting in the way? To improve interactions with others, it is helpful to think of how our styles might be similar or vastly different from theirs. The following sections contain some hints on how to consider altering your style slightly in some areas to have improved communications with others. When you improve the communication process, the chances for increased personal credibility are much stronger!

Direct or Diplomatic?

When dealing with someone who is very *direct*, try flexing your own style so that you do the following:

- Make your point clearly and directly.

- Avoid too much rationalizing or justifying—simply state your thoughts with a degree of confidence and authority.

- Most important, don't assume this person is being harsh or rude. That is rarely the intent of a direct style. Instead, try to remember that this person is merely speaking in the most efficient manner he or she can. Avoid personalizing and stick with the facts.

When dealing with someone whose communication style is less direct and more *diplomatic,* consider the following:

- Be patient. This person is not usually trying to beat around the bush. Work hard at stopping your own thoughts and allow this person to finish expressing himself.

- Watch your vocal tone and body language. Allow the person with the diplomacy style to set the pace and work against demonstrating your desire to move the conversation more quickly.

- Paraphrase or restate what you hear periodically. Say, "So, you are saying that _____," and then try to restate the key points you've heard. This allows you to move the conversation forward and helps the other person stay on track.

- Diplomacy is a strong skill and one valued by many people. Observe how more diplomatic individuals use phrases and words to present thoughts or requests of others in a way that is less likely to ruffle feathers and often generates more commitment from others.

What about you? Are you struggling in a relationship that might be based upon a difference in styles? Is it possible that one of those differences is in this area of **direct or diplomatic**? Think through this relationship, consider your own personal preference and the other individual's likely preference, and then respond to these questions:

- How could each of you benefit from communicating more effectively?

  _____

  _____

  _____

- What could the other person say or do differently that could help this to occur?

  _____

  _____

  _____

- What could you say or do differently that might help?

  _____

  _____

  _____

- What are you going to do to make that happen?

  _____

  _____

  _____

Retreat or Engage?

When interacting with someone who prefers to *retreat* (think and reflect first), consider the following:

- When possible, *schedule* time to talk with that person. Let them know in advance what you want to talk about and set a mutual time for the discussion. This allows the person to be prepared and give advance thought to the topic. You will be amazed at how much more attentive and relaxed he or she will be as a result!

- Be prepared to give your focus to this individual. People who prefer to retreat will always prefer to interact one-on-one versus group settings. Even in a group setting, understand that this person is capable of blocking out all other activities going on around him. So, you are showing that you value that person more when you can also give your focused attention to that individual.

- Pay attention to the energy this person is demonstrating. If you can sense that this person is showing fatigue, understand that he or she has probably had insufficient time alone to retreat and refresh the energy level.

- Try to modify your own body language, vocal tone, and speaking pace so that you are not overwhelming the person who prefers to retreat.

- Ask questions to draw out the thoughts and ideas of someone who prefers to retreat. And, be prepared for this individual to take time to pause, reflect upon your question, and then answer. This usually means that the person is thinking about your question and giving it serious consideration—it does not mean anything other than that. (Don't be tempted to assume anything about what the person might be thinking while silent—odds are that you're wrong!)

When interacting with someone who loves to *engage* with others and demonstrates energy from it, consider the following:

- Self-expression is necessary for this person to survive. So, don't try to shut that down or tune it out.

- Give occasional verbal affirmations such as, "That's right!" or, "Yes, I know!"

- Take the initiative to interject your own thoughts and ideas as they occur. If you don't, you might never have an opportunity to interact!

- After making your thoughts clear, ask, "What are your thoughts?" Your engager will stay engaged. He or she really needs to be able to talk. Keeping the conversation flowing back and forth between the two of you will keep that energy going!

What about you? Are you struggling in a relationship that might be based upon a difference in styles? Is it possible that one of those differences is in this area of **retreat or engage**? Think through this relationship, consider your own personal preference and the other individual's likely preference, and then respond to these questions:

- How could each of you benefit from communicating more effectively?

  _____

  _____

  _____

- What could the other person say or do differently that could help this to occur?

  _____

  _____

  _____

- What could you say or do differently that might help?

  _____

  _____

  _____

- What are you going to do to make that happen?

  _____

  _____

  _____

Options or Plans?

When communicating with someone who prefers to keep many *options* open, prefers to be spontaneous, and resists the idea of a structured plan, consider the following:

- Keep an open mind to leaving options open for discussion for a period of time. Then, if needed, try to gain agreement in advance of when final decisions will be made and the details planned.

- The person who prefers keeping options open also needs to feel that he or she is able to "go with the flow" as things occur. So, if it is not really critical to finalize specific details, don't push toward that. For example, if one person really wants to allow the events of the day to determine the time for dinner that evening, that might be fine. However, feel free to suggest a time that you agree that dinner will occur by. ("Let's agree that we'll not overly plan the day, but that we will shoot for dinner by 8:00 p.m.—how's that?") The person who likes options is usually fine with setting limits— they just resist an environment being overly structured.

- When communicating with someone who needs to keep options open, remain flexible wherever possible. Ask yourself, "Is it more important to drive my structured agenda, or is it more important to remain open, allow spontaneous opportunities, and keep the communication flowing?"

- If you need more structure in life, talk about that. Gain agreement on how you will work together to meet the needs of both individuals. Typically, some areas of life can be well managed without a great deal of structure or plans—and other areas need that structure for tasks to be accomplished.

- Observe the joy and energy of the individual who enjoys keeping life open and flexible. Typically, this is someone who is able to live in the present and, therefore, gains pleasure from the simple, yet important aspects of life. Look for opportunities to apply those same qualities to your life experience!

Some tips for effective communications with the person who is very structured and develops *plans* include the following:

- First, understand that the lack of planning creates a high degree of stress for this individual. So, stress will reduce based on this person's ability to develop that plan. Stress impacts everyone, so allow stress to reduce by accepting this aspect of this individual.

- Dealing with change is typically more difficult for someone who needs plans and structure. You can improve communication with this individual when you consider any changes to previous planning that you might be intentionally or unintentionally creating for this individual. Then, communicate those changes as far in advance as possible. Typically, the person who needs plans will accommodate changes when they feel there is some time to develop "Plan B."

- Observe the benefits of effective planning. Notice the reduced stress that can occur when details are considered in advance and plans are implemented effectively. Learn to value individuals who have this preference, and wherever possible, learn to enjoy the ease in life's details that can occur as a result.

What about you? Are you struggling in a relationship that might be based upon a difference in styles? Is it possible that one of those differences is in this area of *options or plans*? Think through this relationship, consider your own personal preference and the other individual's likely preference, and then respond to these questions:

- How could each of you benefit from communicating more effectively?

  _____

  _____

  _____

- What could the other person say or do differently that could help this to occur?

  _____

  _____

  _____

- What could you say or do differently that might help?

  _____

  _____

  _____

- What are you going to do to make that happen?

  _____

  _____

  _____

Some Final Thoughts on Style Differences and Personal Credibility

As humans, we are each wonderfully and uniquely made. Each of us has our own "special" blend of style preferences and communication. There is no "right" or "wrong" style. Our opportunity is to increase our own personal credibility through knowing ourselves, and then interacting more effectively as a result of that knowledge. It is through this process of gaining factual information and objectivity *about ourselves and then about others* that allows personal credibility to develop and grow. It isn't about trying to be someone or something other than our authentic self, but rather about trying to maximize that authentic self and maximizing relationships with others.

chapter nine

Step #6:
Ask More and Listen Most

Can you imagine this scenario? You are at work. You have just
returned to your desk from a meeting that ran a little late, and you
need to catch up on the day's messages before your next appointment.
So, you press the speaker button on your phone and begin listening to
your many voice mail messages. While you listen to a message that
seems to go on forever, you turn around to your computer and begin
clearing your e-mail, targeting first the junk mail and others that you
know can be immediately deleted. While the speaker phone drones
on, and as you are deleting e-mail messages, a coworker walks up to
your desk and says, "Do you have a minute for a quick question?" Your
immediate response is, "Sure…go ahead," while you continue to
delete voice and e-mail messages. About two minutes later, your
coworker asks you to repeat what she just said. You look at her in
amazement and realize your only response can be, "I have no idea!"
How on Earth could you repeat what she said? There is no way that
you were able to listen!

Whether in the workplace or in our personal lives, technology has "advanced." And, the result of those advancements is often resulting in the decline of our ability to stop, pay attention to the other person, and listen. There is so much competing for our attention—television, radio, and the Internet, to name a few. Many of us have both landline and cellular telephones. You would think the last thing in the world we would be dealing with is ineffective communications!

Think for a moment and consider people who you have come to trust and respect—many of those individuals take the time to stop and listen to others.

They not only listen, but they are able to demonstrate personal credibility through some very specific actions that they take while they listen! Think back to Secret #3, "The Decision to Suspend Judgment." There is another part of that secret that we'll discover here. It is that people who listen carefully are really the only ones who can tap into this secret. There simply is no way to suspend judgment without first being able to shut down our own thoughts for the moment and then focus on listening to the other person.

When we first reviewed the meaning of personal credibility, we found that people who give and receive respect are most likely to have personal credibility. We both show respect and experience the benefit of receiving it as a result of listening. When we make a decision to listen closely, we automatically have a leg up on personal credibility. Furthermore, there are specific tactics that can make a huge difference both in how well we really listen and how others perceive us.

Tip #1:
Stop and Connect

We often take the power of listening for granted. It seems like such a simple, natural thing to do. The problem is exactly that: Because it seems so simple, we can completely lose focus on what is really involved. People who possess strong personal credibility tend to either stop what they are doing and listen—or postpone the conversation until they can take the time to do it.

Think for a moment of how you feel when you are talking and you get the very clear indication that the person you are speaking with is totally checked out.

Maybe you see a yawn being stifled, or perhaps you see eyes glazing over. Typically, you see some type of body language in the other individual that says, "I don't want to listen to you." You feel insulted, right? You probably feel like you are unimportant. Now, if this person is someone you completely trust and respect, you will forgive this lack of listening—for a while. But over time, someone's lack of listening will eventually impact your decision to trust and respect that individual. Most of us find it very difficult to trust and respect someone who indicates a lack of desire to listen.

What is the best way to use this tip on listening? It's actually many little things that add up. The most important steps include the following:

1. Stop other activities.

2. Make eye contact.

3. Show engagement in your body language—nod your head, lean forward, occasionally interject an "Uh-huh" or "I see." Smile when appropriate.

4. Instead of thinking of your response, think in terms of capturing the key points the person is making. Suspend judgment while you are connecting!

Tip #2:
Restate or Paraphrase

Think about some of the best listeners you know.

How do they do it? Most great listeners have trained themselves to use the technique of paraphrasing or restating what they are hearing. These individuals will gently interrupt the conversation from time to time and say things that allow you both to know that you are on the same track. When you hear the listener use his or her own words to summarize or restate what you are saying, you are very clear that this individual is carefully listening to you.

The following tips might help you use the technique of paraphrasing and restating when you are listening:

- At an appropriate gap in the conversation, simply restate or paraphrase what you heard. Some examples might include, "So you're saying that you don't agree with James' point of view?" Or, "If I understand correctly, you want to take a different approach to solving this problem—is that right?" Notice that you are *not* sharing your thoughts or opinions when you restate or paraphrase. You are simply capturing the essence of the other person's statements.

- Paraphrase whenever you are concerned that the person is rambling or moving off point. Gently interrupt and say, "Let me make sure I understand the issue so far. You're saying that…" and then restate what you heard.

- Use paraphrasing as a means of keeping your own emotions in check. How does this happen? It's another example of applying what you learned in Secret #3. If you are listening with the *intent* of being able to restate what you hear— versus offering your own opinion—you will be more likely to suspend judgment for a while. That short while, combined with your ability to paraphrase what you heard, buys your emotions a little time. It is very difficult to get lost in your own thoughts and feelings if you are listening intently with the purpose of being able to paraphrase or restate what you are hearing. In fact, it is almost impossible!

Tip #3:
Ask, Ask, Ask...

When we listen, we are often chomping at the bit for the other person to catch their breath so that we can insert our own thoughts or opinions. Personal credibility is enhanced, however, not necessarily by our jumping in to express our thoughts, but rather by our ability to step back, ask more questions, and better understand the other person.

"Stephanie" and "Ryan" and their family of four teenagers had been living in their home for about two years. The home was in a golf course neighborhood and because Ryan loved playing golf, he was thrilled with their home and neighborhood. Stephanie, however, was not as positive. Before they had built this home and moved in, Stephanie had desperately wanted to build a home on several acres in a more rural setting. They didn't find the right property quickly, and because Ryan wanted to make a decision and move on, Stephanie agreed to the golf course neighborhood plan. When they built their home, it was one of the first homes in the new neighborhood. Then, other houses started to fill in the empty lots. Stephanie could not get her dream out of her mind of where she really wanted to live. On occasion, Stephanie would say something like, "I want to talk about building another home with more acreage." Ryan's response was always about the same, "We just built this home! This is fine! I don't want to talk about another home!" He simply wasn't open to discussing it. Stephanie would get her feelings hurt, shut down, and decide to drop it, but nothing was really resolved.

Finally, Stephanie decided to try asking more questions of Ryan. It was their daily habit to walk for exercise each morning before going to work. One day while on a walk, Stephanie asked Ryan, *"Can you help me understand why you are not willing to discuss* the possibility of building another home on several acres?" Ryan was more willing to explain his position when he was *asked* to explain his thoughts. He quickly listed several reasons. Ryan said, "I'm close to my office at this location. I don't want to move and drive a further distance every day, and we know that we were not able to find property we like close by." Stephanie would then listen and *not* offer her thoughts (that's the tough part!) She just said, "That's fair. *Is there anything else that bothers you about talking about it?*" Ryan responded with, "Stephanie, I don't mind talking about it, but I just don't see the point." Stephanie laughed a little and said, "You're struggling seeing the point of it, I can tell. It is important to me, so, *would you mind if we could just talk a little more about it?*" Ryan, who didn't want to be unreasonable, agreed to allow the conversation to go forward. Stephanie said, "You don't want to drive further to work every day. *What else concerns you about* looking again for property?" Over several days of these walks and occasional discussions, Stephanie continued asking, and Ryan listed several valid reasons for his position: With four teens at home, he wanted to be able to leave his office and check in periodically on the kids and keep appropriate supervision of their activities while both he and Stephanie were at work. He enjoyed the golf club and wanted to stay involved. He did not want to significantly increase their financial obligation with a larger mortgage.

Stephanie just kept listening and asking Ryan to help her understand his concerns. She didn't debate him, nor object to those concerns. She did, however, after asking questions and listening closely on many occasions, eventually *ask* if Ryan would be willing to hear her reasons for looking again for a different location for their home. It would have been difficult for Ryan to refuse—he had been respectfully asked and listened to about this issue for a while. She asked Ryan to just hear her out and think about what she said without interrupting as she had been willing to do. So, he agreed to listen. Stephanie then provided her reasons, which included that the golf course neighborhood was growing into a much larger development than originally planned. As a result, traffic was becoming a problem coming in and out of the neighborhood. She and Ryan loved the outdoors and natural beauty, but as the neighborhood grew, all they were seeing were more houses squeezed closely together. There were some design issues with their house that were causing some space problems with their family. They lived fast-paced, hectic lives, and she yearned for the peace that would come from living in a more secluded area.

Finally, Stephanie asked a very important question: "Ryan, *would you be willing* to look again for a different location for our home if we could find something that would allow you a similar commute to work and home, and also would not stretch our financial commitment beyond what we're comfortable with?" Ryan pointed out that their past efforts had failed, but finally agreed to give it another try. They both agreed that this was not urgent—they would take their time and keep an open mind. A few months later, they found several wooded acres located within an easy drive to Ryan's office, built a beautiful home on it, and both Ryan and Stephanie have enjoyed all aspects of living there for many years now.

This story demonstrates the power of asking questions. Stephanie needed to be able to fully discuss the situation, but Ryan wasn't willing to talk about it. By her asking more and listening carefully, the couple was able to fully explore the situation and come to a conclusion that was workable for both. Ryan often says today that he was helped by Stephanie's questions—they helped him define his concerns in his own mind. They also helped him to explore his own objections and decide which issues were "deal breakers" and which were not. Stephanie learned that communications will open up through asking questions, listening closely to responses, paraphrasing, and then asking more. She learned the power of suspending her own judgment to understand Ryan's concerns. Now, be assured, this is effective only when the questions are legitimate and authentic. Stephanie didn't ask questions to "trap" Ryan into changing his mind or to debate with him. She asked questions to gain more information and understanding.

Secret #3—the decision to suspend judgment—is not always an easy task. However, when we decide to *ask more and listen most*, we are much more likely to tap into the power of that secret. When we listen and ask questions, we are showing genuine interest in the other person.

When we work to fully understand others and can demonstrate that we do, we are increasing personal credibility.

chapter ten

Step #7:
Create Credible Interactions

We have explored how effective listening and questioning can help you tap into Secret #3, "The Decision to Suspend Judgment." The reality is that when we are able to interact in such a way that builds trust and respect, we naturally build personal credibility. We'll go back to a few examples of individuals who have previously been introduced. We can learn a lot about credible interactions by evaluating a few of their successful techniques.

Interaction Technique: Maximize Your Agreements

Have you ever had a conversation with someone where you ended up more confident of your own thoughts and ideas at the end of the discussion?

This often happens when you are talking with someone who is effective in the way he or she *agrees* with you. You might be thinking: Agreement with someone doesn't seem like a big deal! Why does this even register on the interaction radar scale? It's because agreements give us the chance to assure people that we are on the same page—and do this in a way that actually allows them to understand *why* it is so. Agreement situations are maximized when we both acknowledge the fact that we are in agreement—and explain why or how it matters.

If you recall, "Alice" was a member of a senior management group of an organization. Although she certainly did not agree with everything her team members suggested or believed, she was very effective at finding points of agreement and maximizing the impact of those agreements.

"Joanna" was another member of the leadership team. Joanna had the reputation of being a contrarian—she often found an opposite way of looking at information, and sometimes it seemed she did this just for the sake of argument or debate among team members. However, Joanna was extremely smart and her "opposing" viewpoints were important ones to consider and discuss. Alice used the technique of maximizing agreement very effectively with Joanna. Alice would say something like this, "Joanna, I *agree* with the need to explore the possible downsides of this idea *because* we need to be sure we don't overly invest in it without fully analyzing it." This was a credible interaction—both with Joanna and the rest of the team. The team would then move forward with a factual discussion.

"Joe" was another leader on the team. Joe was a realist and often resisted overly aggressive project deadlines and dates. He believed the organization tried to bite off more than it could realistically chew. Alice would listen, seeking points of agreement, and then make comments such as, "Joe, *I agree* that we need to make sure we have realistic target dates *because* there are other projects that will be impacted by these dates." Please don't misunderstand this technique. This is not manipulation or "kissing up"—the old Human Invisible Fence Antennae (HIFA) will activate pretty quickly when someone is doing that. It's simply taking a statement such as, "I agree" or "You're right" a slight step further by explaining *why*.

When you take the time to put words around the why of your agreement, you are able to increase credibility in your interactions. You help both yourself and the other individual understand the value of the interaction.

Interaction Technique:
Create Productive Disagreements

Without a doubt, our personal credibility is probably more challenged when we disagree with someone. Our ability to avoid relying on our position or status, remain transparent, and simultaneously suspend judgment can be quite difficult. Our human emotions enter the picture, we feel the need to defend our beliefs or values, and the next thing you know we are engaged in an interaction that can damage the relationship. When the relationship is damaged and left without repair, we can lose respect. When we lose respect, we lose personal credibility.

Yet, life's reality says that we do not always agree with everyone and everything. Credibility is often built or destroyed based on this reality. Some people handle disagreement through aggressive verbal attacks toward the person with whom they disagree. Others avoid the person with whom they disagree, and often carry a great deal of resentment and anger as a result. Neither of these options increases the opportunity for improved relationships and increased credibility. The option of *productive disagreement* does both. Productive disagreement is a simple, three-step process:

1. ***Identify the value of the other person's point of view.***
   This requires that we stop and seriously consider the other person's beliefs and perspective. When we disagree with that perspective, this can be the most challenging aspect of the productive disagreement process. But, everyone has some reason for his or her perspective. You can always find the value if you are willing to listen and consider it. If nothing else, there is value in their right to have a different opinion! You can use phrases like, "I can see that you believe…" or, "I agree with your thoughts on…." Using this language helps both of the people involved in the disagreement find common ground.

2. **Identify your concerns.** Please note that this is not about just giving in and giving up. That would create no lasting results and probably leave negative impact on your credibility. When you just give up and give in without truly meaning it, you lose self-respect, and others typically follow suit fairly quickly. Instead, simply state your concerns in an objective manner. You might say, "What concerns me is…" or, "The obstacle I see is…." Notice you are not using the word disagree, but instead are listing concerns, obstacles, or barriers that might be in the way.

3. **Discuss ways to maintain the value of the other person's perspective while eliminating or resolving your concerns.** When you genuinely respect the other person's perspective or at least their right to it, and have addressed your concerns, you are then able to move on to problem solving. This process should involve both parties and be mutual. You might ask, "How can we get what you need, yet address my concerns?" or, "What are your ideas for getting what you need, yet overcoming the obstacles I see?" When the other person is unable to offer suggestions at the moment, be prepared with a thought. You can say, "What if we…" and then complete the sentence in a way that might address the other person's issue as well as your concerns. At bare minimum, you can always suggest that the two of you brainstorm ideas for doing that.

The opportunity for engaging in productive disagreements occurs for most of us every day. Review the following scenarios and you will learn that this process can fit naturally into any disagreement you may face.

Scenario #1:
There's More Than One Way to Look at Numbers

"Chuck" is a chief financial officer of a major corporation. He is leading the budget-planning process for the company for the following year. This can be a contentious process for everyone because, typically, each department head wants to plan increased spending, and the profit margin could be negatively impacted. Chuck's role is to lead the entire group toward reasonable spending plans that allow profitability. Chuck and "Ray," the head of IT (Information Technology), are disagreeing on Ray's plan for spending for his IT group. Ray is getting frustrated because it appears that Chuck is not willing to consider his perspective. Then, Ray utilizes productive disagreement as a technique for resolving the disagreement.

Chuck: *"Ray, there is no way that we can spend what you are planning on new technology. I cannot see where these planned expenditures will help us increase sales, and they could drain our profits if we move forward at the pace you are recommending. This is just not feasible."*

Ray (identifies the value of Chuck's position): *"I know that your role is to ensure that this organization is following a sound financial plan for both maintaining our current business and growing new business, Chuck. You must ensure our profitability."*

Chuck: *"Well, I'm glad for that—I wasn't sure you understood that when I saw your spending recommendations!"*

Ray (identifies his concerns): *"I do, Chuck. What concerns me is that I believe we actually will be losing profits by this time next year if we are not able to respond more quickly to customer demands for certain information. New technology will allow us to meet those needs."*

Chuck: *"Okay, but...like I said, we can't spend like this!"*

Ray   (discusses ways to maintain the value of Chuck's per-
          spective while eliminating or resolving his concerns):
          *"What if we agreed to review the entire IT spending
          plan and find ways to possibly decrease spending in
          other areas so that we could reconsider investing in the
          new technology, which might help us with customer
          retention?"*

Chuck: *"If you can do that, then we can talk about the tech-
          nology investment further. I'm glad that you under-
          stand the business reality of this."*

Next is an example of productive disagreement that might be a little
closer to home!

Scenario #2:
She Was Always Late!

Remember "Roy"? He was the man with two prior marriages. If you recall, Roy's style was to communicate very directly, which resulted in hurt feelings and damaged relationships. Roy has had a successful third marriage. He learned that relationships could benefit a great deal from greater self-awareness as well as applying productive disagreement techniques.

Roy was becoming somewhat frustrated because his wife, "Jan," always seemed to be running late. If they agreed to meet at the theater for a movie at 6:00 p.m., she would usually arrive five to ten minutes late. If they were to leave the house by 9:30 a.m. to go to church, she was rushing out of the house at 9:35. Roy knew that if he did not address the issue effectively, he would likely address it ineffectively and create a problem. So, he chose the productive disagreement route!

Roy:	*"Jan, I need to talk about something that's bothering me. Is now OK?"*
Jan:	*"Sure, but please don't get on me about being late. I just couldn't help it! Roy, I just wish you could be a little more flexible and not so darn time-sensitive!"*
Roy	(identifies the value of Jan's perspective): *"I know that you don't want to have an argument or debate about this. I don't want to be inflexible and I want you to know that."*
Jan:	*"That's good! Sometimes, you are little nuts about timeliness!"*
Roy	(identifies his concerns): *"(chuckles) I might be that. What concerns me is that we aren't talking about something that could create some problems for us if we don't come up with a mutual way to resolve it."*
Jan:	*"Well, OK, I guess we can talk about it, but I just couldn't help what happened with being late today!"*

Roy   (continues identifying his concerns): *"I'm becoming more and more frustrated each time you are late. You seem to be getting more stressed out also."*

Jan: *"Yes, I know you're frustrated, and you are definitely right about my getting more stressed. I don't want to be late, but unexpected things happen and then I really get stressed because I know you are getting angry. It's a double whammy!"*

Roy   (discusses ways to maintain the value of Jan's perspective and resolve his concerns): *"How about we talk about some ways that could reduce the stress you're dealing with, but also reduce the frustration I feel when it causes us to be late?"*

Jan: *"Well, I'm all for that... ."* (This conversation can now move forward in a problem-solving mode.)

Both Ray and Roy had something to lose if they did not handle these disagreements well. However, both situations needed to be addressed. The question we need to ask ourselves is this: How can I discuss what is happening in a way that has a productive versus destructive outcome? There definitely is some effort involved in having a productive disagreement. Usually, the results we receive are well worth the effort expended. When we are able to have productive disagreements, we enhance our self-respect. We also enhance the respect others have for us. We increase personal credibility.

Interaction Technique: Express Your Thoughts with Credibility

People who have strong personal credibility usually *sound* credible when they speak. This does not imply that everyone who speaks well is credible. You might not need to look much further than the political arena to understand that although there are many effective speakers, not everyone is someone who you respect and trust. However, individuals who possess the ability to express thoughts and ideas effectively are able to gain respect with greater ease than those who don't. The good news is that everyone can positively impact their own personal credibility factor by focusing on a few basic speaking components.

Effective speaking or expression involves three components:
- ***Who** am I speaking to?*
- ***What** am I saying?*
- ***How** do I say it most effectively?*

Who Am I Speaking To?

Most of us open our mouths, begin to speak, and our main focus is telling others what we think. Individuals who speak with greater credibility often think first of their audience, and then what they will say. Even if it is an audience of one, we become more credible when we think about who is listening to us, consider their issues and needs, and then focus our message to meet those needs. We actually do this in many situations already. Think of your last discussion with your grandparents or a senior citizen. Typically, you are less likely to speak about things that are not relevant to the lives of an older adult. If the older adult is not overly familiar with computers and technology, odds are that you would not launch into a discussion of how you applied a new software package to help you in your business. You might say that you were helped by a new software package, but you would likely avoid going into the details of the technology. You are being sensitive to your listener and customizing what you say. If you are talking with someone in the Information Technology field, however, your discussion might be completely different about that new software package.

We can also tie being sensitive to our listeners with communication styles and preferences. We are so much more effective when we consider who we are speaking with along with how that person best receives information. For example, when dealing with someone who seeks retreat in interactions, we might begin a discussion with, "You'll probably want to think about this and consider it for a while." This will immediately allow the listener to relax, knowing that you understand the need to think internally first before they offer ideas and thoughts. All of this can occur very quickly and does not need to be mechanical or awkward. We can do it automatically and without much thought when we develop the desire to express ourselves with credibility and form the habit of considering listeners and their needs first.

What Am I Saying?

Speaking with credibility also involves the ability to make a point with clarity. When we organize our thoughts slightly in advance, we can gain the attention of the listener quickly, and hold their attention longer. Organization is actually pretty simple. When we begin speaking, it's more effective when we

1. Begin with our main or key point.
2. Next, offer supporting points.
3. Finally, summarize our message in closing.

When we organize the content of our message in this simple way, we speak with greater credibility. If we know the main point we are making, and we know the points that offer support for that main point, we are less likely to ramble in our communications. Our listeners can immediately sense that we have a plan, and they will typically retain interest in hearing us out. When we are interrupted in the conversation, we can always return to our main point, and then pick up again on making supporting points about that.

After we have made our main point, then offered our supporting points, it is often effective to offer a quick summary of what we said. When a conversation has been interrupted and dialogue has occurred, this can be extremely critical to creating credible interactions. Through summarization, we leave the listener with a clear understanding of our message, and lay the groundwork for moving forward. We have spoken in a way that communicates intentional thought, organization, and helps the listener remember our message.

How Do I Say It Effectively?

In reality, we can consider our listener or audience, provide a message that is concise and logical in content, and still blow it on the credibility scale. This occurs because of issues or problems with our manner of delivering the message. Delivery includes our tone of voice, body language, and other signals that either create or destroy credibility from the listener's perspective. We are naturally more credible when others see us as being confident and comfortable when we speak. Attention to a few details can often remove barriers to credibility. Consider the following checklist in evaluating your own effectiveness on delivering messages.

Complete the following checklist, rating yourself with the following scale:

1 = Always

2 = Sometimes

3 = Rarely

4 = Never

Body Language:

_____ My posture is confident. My shoulders are back, and my head is up.

_____ I maintain a positive, relaxed facial expression.

_____ I use gestures to emphasize what I say.

_____ I avoid overuse of gestures or allowing my hands to become distracting when I speak.

_____ If nervous, I place my shaky or jittery hands where neither others nor I can see them. I keep them there until the jitters pass.

_____ I move around in an intentional manner if needed. I avoid pacing around or moving randomly.

Eye Contact:

_____ I maintain eye contact with the person I am speaking with.

_____ When speaking to groups, I move my eyes around the group, making eye contact with everyone who is involved. I make sure I have made an eye connection with someone before moving my eyes to the next person.

_____ I speak to people when I read information aloud, not to the paper or document I'm reading from. I vary my eye contact from the document to the listeners.

Voice/Vocal Tone:

_____ I pace the words I speak intentionally. I work at speaking neither too quickly nor too slowly.

_____ I intentionally slow down my pace of speech when I am feeling nervous.

_____ I modify my vocal tone to accentuate the points I make. I emphasize excitement or other emotions in my voice so that the listener can quickly identify and relate to what I say.

_____ I am sensitive to the volume of my voice. I clarify that others can hear me and then adjust my volume of speaking accordingly.

The following is an example of how making some slight adjustments to her style of delivery impacted one young woman's credibility factor.

"Lynn" works for a local university. She meets and speaks regularly with incoming college freshman through one-on-one conversations, as well as makes frequent presentations about the university's services and programs during freshman orientation. Lynn is smart and very articulate. Even though she is in her mid-thirties, she looks much younger and could easily pass for a teenager. Most of us would consider youthful appearance a good thing, but it was actually working against Lynn. She had a difficult time gaining the attention of her student listeners. She knew intuitively that she was not perceived by these students with the degree of respect that was needed for her role with the university. Lynn decided to do something about it.

First, Lynn invited a friend whom she trusted to sit in on some of her student interviews and presentations. She asked her friend to give her feedback and ideas on how she might adjust her delivery style so that she could gain more attention and respect from the students. As a result of her friend's insights as well as her own analysis, Lynn made a few adjustments, including the following:

- ***Slower paced speech patterns***—Lynn deliberately slowed down. Most younger students were accustomed to speaking very rapidly. Lynn simply moved in the opposite direction with her pacing, which quickly set her aside as being "different."

- ***Controlled body language***—Lynn noticed that many students tend to move a lot, use hand movements frequently, shift in their seats, and generally demonstrate some degree of uncontrolled energy. Lynn adjusted her body movements. She moved more deliberately, and consciously used more erect posture. Lynn noticed a change in response from students almost instantly. They seemed to be more calm and attentive.

- **Sustained eye contact**—Lynn realized that she needed to capture the interest of students who were easily distracted and often looking everywhere but at her. She did this with unrelenting eye contact. In doing this, she quickly commanded the attention of both individuals and groups.

- **Image adjustment**—Although not directly connected with our verbal ability of presenting thoughts and ideas, our personal image is a part of what we communicate about ourselves. Lynn needed to shift her personal image just enough to have students perceive her as being more mature. She made some slight wardrobe adjustments, and chose clothing for work that sent a more serious message. She chose to dress like an adult instead of dressing as a young college student. That, along with these other adjustments, allowed Lynn to remove unwanted barriers to her personal credibility.

Lynn needed to gain more respect when she spoke. She needed to be perceived as a more mature adult to gain the respect from her student audience. Other situations might require that we lighten up just a bit and go the other direction to relate more effectively with our audience. If we first consider *who* we are speaking with, we can then make the decisions about what we say and how we say it more effectively.

Now, don't panic! It is not a requirement that you be a polished, professional speaker to gain and increase your personal credibility factor. However, if you can take just a few seconds to think first about your listener, then the key point of your message, and focus on an effective delivery of that message, you can increase your own speaking skills while positively impacting your credibility factor at the same time. When you speak, others will want to listen!

Part III

Face the Truth
and
Begin Anew

chapter eleven

The Truth Shall Set You Free—
When You Avoid Truth Traps!

We know inherently that we lose trust in others when they are not truthful with us. We can also easily understand that others lose trust in us when we are less than truthful. Yet, if we are *honest*, we can agree that we all get caught up in some truth "traps" from time to time. Some might have a more devastating impact on our personal credibility factor than we are aware. If we can learn to identify those common truth traps and learn proactive strategies for avoiding them, we can protect our personal credibility factor to a greater degree.

Trap #1:
The Little White Lie

Most people are familiar with this trap. It seems so innocent, actually. It happens when we tell someone something that we believe will be less likely to hurt their feelings, while at the same time trying to protect ourselves from being judged by that person. You might identify with some of the following examples:

- You are invited to dinner at the home of an acquaintance. Your last experience with dinner at this person's house was a disaster. Suffice it to say that culinary arts are not a blessing at this household! Additionally, you find the spouse of this person very obnoxious. You don't want to go, but you obviously must explain why without hurting feelings, right? So, you just invent another engagement for the evening, explaining that you already have dinner plans with your sister. You forget about it. Then, at the last minute, you decide to eat out with some friends at a local restaurant. Guess who you run into at that restaurant? You guessed it—your less-than-culinary-gifted acquaintance! *Trapped!*

- A neighbor has decided to host a gathering to say good-bye to other neighbors who are moving out of town. You are exhausted because of your recent busy schedule. Although you had indicated that you would attend, you just can't muster up the energy when the day comes. So, you cancel, telling the hostess that you have been feeling sick all day and, unfortunately, can't attend. All's well, right? Well, yes, except that when other neighbors attend, one friend shares several funny stories from your afternoon golf outing that same day. When the hostess says, "I'm so sorry Nick couldn't make it tonight, he said he'd been sick all day!" Your golfing buddy says, "Well, he seemed fine today on the golf course!" *Trapped!*

- Your son and daughter-in-law give you a gift for your birthday. You already have the exact item, but don't want to hurt their feelings and not show appreciation. So, you graciously say thanks and later inquire about where they purchased the gift, stating that you would like to possibly purchase another item that would match it. The next week, you take the gift back to the store to return it. While waiting in the return line holding the gift, your daughter-in-law walks in and walks up to see you! She notices you holding the gift she had given you and looks at you with a questioning expression. *Trapped!*

Trap #2:
The Need to Be "In the Know"

Another truth trap occurs when we are interacting with someone and they assume we know more about a topic than we actually do. When this happens, we sometimes find ourselves innocently right in the middle of some juicy gossip or information that we have not previously had access to. We can become trapped in this situation as a result of our failing to stop the conversation and clarify that this is new information and we have no prior knowledge.

Consider this example: The senior management group of your organization has been discussing various alternatives for decreasing expenses for the upcoming year. As part of the discussion, some departmental review of possible layoffs has occurred. You report to a member of senior management, but have had no access to this situation or information about anything being planned. Then, one of your boss's peers approaches you to discuss "more details about planned cuts" in your department. You allow the conversation to continue, listening and responding in a way that suggests that you are already "in the know." You certainly don't want to appear dumb or uninformed. And, finding this out now could help you personally. Later, this same member of senior management reveals to your boss that you and he had a discussion about departmental cuts—and your boss quickly says, "He doesn't know anything about these discussions about possible layoffs. We are only in the brainstorming mode at this point. How could he have known? And, he certainly never discussed what he knew with me, and I'm his boss!" *Trapped!*

Trap #3:
Loose Lips Sink Ships...and Our Credibility

We have already discussed the devastating effect that participation in gossip or breaking confidences can have on our personal credibility. Using discretion about what we say is critical—even when we are telling the truth. During times of battle or war, extreme caution is taken to ensure that the enemy does not learn about plans for an upcoming battle. A battalion of ships arriving in a harbor to surprise the enemy is useless if word has leaked about that plan in advance. Rather than being placed in a position of power and leverage, the attacker can become the attacked. *Trapped!* There are similar situations we face in other aspects of our lives.

Why do people sometimes have "loose lips"? What causes us to spill the beans at times when it is neither necessary nor appropriate? Usually, it is our own desire to be viewed as having power or influence. We can gain attention and sometimes personal power when we are viewed as someone with "the scoop." When we give into this desire, we ultimately lose credibility as a result, however. We are viewed as being someone who just cannot manage sensitive information, and will eventually become someone whom people avoid sharing anything with. Loose lips can also occur simply as a result of human error—we speak before we think. Regardless of the motive or situation, loose lips are a definite truth trap. Technically, we are speaking the truth. However, if we become involved, we're trapped!

Trap #4:
Don't Worry...It's Done!

Your spouse asks if you remembered to drop off the dirty dry cleaning. Although the clothing is actually out in your car trunk and you plan on going in the morning, you say, "It's all taken care of."

Your boss asks if you have returned the call to your coworker to discuss how you will handle covering work schedules during the holidays. You have actually forgotten, but know you can do it tomorrow and are sure it will work out. So, you say, "I left a message earlier. Don't worry, it's done." Or, a customer asks if you have mailed his account summary as you committed to doing during your conversation three days ago. You say, "Sure did…it's been done!" And then, you actually produce and put the statement in the mail that day.

Each of these situations will likely go by without you actually getting caught in a trap. If you follow through on the dry cleaners the next day, what difference does it really make? If you contact your coworker after talking with your boss and arrange your holiday schedule coverage, why be concerned? If the customer gets his statement as requested, isn't that all that really matters? The reality is this: Each of these situations has considerable opportunities to catch us in a self-made trap. The spouse can be searching for something in your car and accidentally discover the dry cleaning in the trunk. Your boss and coworker can connect before you talk with your coworker, and the boss will learn that no message has been left. The customer might be keeping records of dates/times of interactions with you and realize that the statement you had promised three days prior was postmarked after the second conversation with you to remind you about his request. *Trapped!*

Yes, we can be caught in a trap. Or, we can sometimes escape from the trap without any evidence of our lack of truthfulness. Even when we escape the trap on a single incident, we are impacted internally. One of two things happens: We feel horrible about it, admit our error to ourselves, and resolve to avoid it in the future. Or, we get by with it, which makes it much easier to fall into the same truth trap again. Eventually, though, we all fall into traps when we avoid the truth. And, whether we are aware of it or not, we lose our self-respect, at a minimum.

Truth Trap Tips

Without believing that we are blatantly lying or being overtly dishon-est, we can fall into some truth traps. And, when we do, we stand to lose personal credibility. So, let's review how to avoid these traps.

#1: Make the *Decision* to Be a Truthful Person

This might seem pretty self-evident. Who would decide *not* to be a truthful person? Or, who would actually admit it if they had? The real-ity is that many of us fall into these various truth traps because we haven't given enough advance thought to being truthful. Do you value truth? Do you value those whom you can depend upon to be truthful and honest with you? The decision is each of ours. Avoiding truth traps often begins with first making this decision. The decision to be a truthful person is a deep and personal decision. It is at the core of our personal values and beliefs. However, our beliefs and values are shown to others by our *actions*. Our actions will eventually demon-strate the degree to which we have made the decision to be a truthful person. And, our actions are what will keep us from falling into diffi-cult truth traps. It is from our actions that we gain—or lose—person-al credibility.

#2: Don't Overexplain or Create Excuses— Just Stick with the Facts!

If you need to decline an invitation, you are not obligated to give details about the reasons. A simple "I'm sorry, I can't make it" is all you need to say. If you receive a gift that duplicates something you already have, simply say, "I love it—and so much that I already have one!" Then, ask how you might return it. Let the conversation flow from there. Your desire to share more information or even make a little of it up isn't really about avoiding hurting the other person's feelings. It is more likely that you are more concerned about what this person will think about you. Your honest responses over time increase credibility.

#3: If You Are Clueless...Say So!

If you are hearing information that is new to you but that the speaker believes you know, stop the conversation and let the person know that you have not been informed about it. If you continue to hear information and have made it clear that you have not been previously informed, make sure the appropriate people hear *from you* that you have been given information that might or might not have been designed for your ears. There is no value judgment placed on you for having no previous knowledge—but there can be extreme judgment placed on you if you receive knowledge and then handle the information incorrectly. Your personal credibility regarding appropriate handling of information can either be positively or negatively impacted based on your actions. Long-term personal credibility is more valuable than any short-term desire to be "in the know."

#4: The Truth Doesn't Need Stretching—It Just Needs Doing

It's not a crime to forget something. You are not a bad person if you need more time to accomplish a task than originally planned. You have not failed when you have an occasional dropped ball. However, if you try to pass it off as a task being done or taken care of when that is not factual, you can expect this practice to eventually be discovered. Far better to just say, "Not yet—but I'll get right on it" than to attempt to appear competent while simultaneously revealing a tendency toward covering up facts or stretching the truth.

Truth traps are a part of our everyday life. Most appear harmless when we first discover them. However, if we are not aware of their existence, we might become trapped.
Staying out of traps begins with a decision to be truthful, then proactively developing personal habits and strategies for avoiding those traps in the first place.

chapter twelve

Credibility:
I've Lost It—
Can I Rebuild It?

Perhaps one or more chapters of this book have left you thinking, "I have really blown my personal credibility factor, but what can I do about it now?"

The reality is this: You can rebuild credibility, and if done in a sincere and effective manner, you can even become more credible as a result of blowing it!

Many of us are familiar with customer service situations that were seriously blown by someone, but the way in which the problem was corrected caused us to think even more positively about the experience than we might have if the problem had not occurred in the first place.

Take, for instance, the example of "Elizabeth." Elizabeth is a trainer and speaker who travels for her clients around the country to provide seminars that are held in conference hotels. Elizabeth always closes her seminars with a personal story about how she has overcome her tendency to think negatively about difficult circumstances. To illustrate her point, she tells a story about planting "corn" (positive things) into her mind versus "poison" (negative things). As a visual reminder, each seminar participant is provided a packet of corn seeds that are distributed by the hotel staff before the session begins on the second day. Recently, during a program at a large New York City hotel, Elizabeth noticed that the staff had not distributed the corn seed packets as expected. She brought it to the attention of the staff and requested that the corn be distributed during the lunch break that afternoon. When she returned from lunch, Elizabeth saw small brown paper sacks at each participant's seat instead of the corn seed packets. The hotel's meeting manager approached her immediately and explained that apparently the corn seed packets had been mistakenly thrown out the previous night. When they realized the mistake, a staff member ran to a local market and purchased over 100 paper sacks and packages of microwave popcorn. The staff worked feverishly filling the paper sacks with (pop)corn and then distributed them while the group had lunch. The customer service "mistake" actually turned into an amazing story of problem solving and positive service in this situation. Had the mistake not occurred (throwing away the corn seed packets), the impressive service would not have been so strongly noticed. This same type of opportunity exists for us each time we lose personal credibility—if we respond with positive action to the opportunity!

Rebuilding Is a Process, Not an Event

Two sisters, "Carrie" and "Amy," grew up in a family that struggled in many ways, especially financially. Their father, "Joe," had a difficult time staying employed. Joe was a bit of a dreamer, always seeking the next opportunity to make the big time—usually involving some type of get-rich-quick scheme that he tried and that failed. Joe's wife, "Pam," was constantly looking for ways to feed her children and stretch the family dollar. Pam would work full-time during the day as a cafeteria worker in the public school system. Then, after making sure that her daughters had some type of evening meal, would leave home again, take the bus to another part of town, and work evenings in a retail department store. Meanwhile, Joe generally didn't work, hung out with his buddies, and often cost the family even more money as a result of spending Pam's hard-earned paychecks on the newest scheme or idea that would not work.

Because of so many financial pressures, the marriage experienced a great deal of stress. Joe and Pam fought regularly, and, finally, Joe decided to leave his wife and daughters. He told himself, "I'm not appreciated, and I don't need all this hassle!" After packing his bags, Joe left home in the middle of the night, leaving a short note that said, "I'm out of here. You won't miss me anyway." He did not contact his wife or daughters for over 12 years.

Not surprisingly, Joe's life didn't improve much after he left. He would move in and out of shelters for the homeless; then, after securing a job and earning a few paychecks, he overextended himself financially with credit. His life was in ongoing chaos. However, his wife and daughters were able to pull together and pull through. Pam continued working both jobs, was able to receive several promotions in her retail job, eventually was promoted into a buyer position, and, ultimately, became the leader of the organization's buying operations for the region. Carrie and Amy finished school with excellent grades, and both received scholarships to state universities. Both were young women well on their way to successful and productive lives. Each had her own view of her father, and each had some scars from the devastation that comes from being abandoned by a parent.

On one of his many stays at a homeless shelter, Joe met an amazing counselor and social worker, "Don." For some reason, Don saw potential for goodness in Joe and decided to try to help Joe change the course of his life. Through many long, soul-searching conversations with Don, Joe began dealing with the many mistakes he had made in his life, and most troubling of all, his abandonment of his daughters and wife. Don helped Joe see that the only way he would regain self-respect was to take the right action with his former family. Yes, it would be difficult. Yes, they might be uninterested in seeing him or talking with him after all these years. Yes, he might be rejected. Yes, he could see why his family might not trust him again.

But, if nothing else, he could make the choice to pursue his self-respect and personal credibility.

Nothing positive could happen without his action. And, if nothing else, he would be able to assure himself that he had made an effort.

Joe first contacted his wife, Pam. Pam was very clear that she had no interest in any conversation with Joe. She informed him that because he had been basically missing for over 12 years that she had obtained a legal divorce. Pam asked that Joe not contact her again and that he not make contact with their daughters. She said, "You've done enough damage to their lives. Don't do more now!" That was tough for Joe to hear, but he made the decision to pursue contact with his daughters. He assured Pam that he wanted nothing from them in return; he just wanted to make sure they knew that he was totally wrong in what he had done and would forever regret it.

Joe's daughters responded to him in their own way. The eldest, Carrie, emotionally told Joe that she had no father. Her father had walked out on her family 12 years ago. She didn't need a father and she didn't need his apologies. Joe's response was a quiet, "I know that you have every right to feel this way. What I did was so wrong. I don't expect you to forgive me. I just want you to know that I have truly learned how wrong I have been all these years."

Amy, the younger daughter, had a slightly different response to Joe's contact with her. She was reserved and listened. She only said, "I have no idea how I feel about you. I'll have to think about it." Joe left Amy with information on how she could reach him and said he would appreciate any form of contact with her, even if it was an occasional postcard.

For the next three years, Joe continued working on repairing his life. He found a job with an organization that would partially pay for college tuition. He enrolled in school and pursued a degree in psychology. He worked with Don on a volunteer basis at the shelter, hoping to help others in the way Don had helped him. He regularly sent letters to his daughters, updating them on his changed lifestyle, occasionally sending a photograph of him working at the shelter. He informed them about his upcoming college graduation event and invited them to attend. In his letters, he wrote detailed descriptions of his mistakes, what he had learned from those mistakes, and how he was working to change his life for the better. He also invited them to contact him if they desired, assuring each of his daughters that he understood why they might not be willing to do so.

On the day Joe received his degree, his daughter Amy showed up for the ceremony. When she found her father after the program, she met him with tears glistening in her eyes. She simply said, "I'd like to have you in my life." Joe told her that nothing could mean more to him, and he would treasure any opportunity to know his daughter. Over the next year, Amy and Joe became father and daughter, as well as very good friends. Amy also became involved in the shelter with Don, and Don, Joe, and Amy were able to open a second location in a very needy area of town.

Carrie has chosen not to open her life up to her father. She is aware of the relationship that Amy has with her dad and often marvels that it can happen. Joe continues to send letters and cards to Carrie, with the hope that someday she might decide to consider opening herself up to him. He still has no expectations; he just simply knows that he is the one who needs to make the effort. His self-respect is built upon it. His credibility is being rebuilt based upon it.

A Simple Statement: "You Were Right"

Not all losses and rebuilding processes of personal credibility are as dramatic as the one with Joe and his family. Remember "Lynn"? She is the young woman who worked for a university and struggled with gaining the respect of students who considered her to be "just one of them," leading her to realize she needed to change a few things to gain personal credibility with the students. Lynn works with "Becky." Becky is a long-time employee at the university and can be difficult for her fellow employees to deal with. She is frequently critical, openly challenging their ideas and suggestions when the team meets for departmental meetings. It is very common for Becky to say, "That will never work" or, "You don't have the same level of experience I have— you are not doing that right!" Lynn is very organized and thorough in her work, especially in times of student enrollment. She understands that details can easily slip through the cracks, and that the result of that occurring can be time consuming and expensive for students who might be on the receiving end of the university staff's errors. Becky was openly critical of Lynn's approach to an upcoming student orientation, telling her she was spending time and energy unnecessarily, and that no matter how much she planned, there would be mistakes made and there was nothing that could be done.

Thanks to Lynn's planning, the orientation went more smoothly than any previous student orientation processes. Becky observed this. And, she did a remarkable thing. She approached Lynn and said, "You were right in your approach and planning of this orientation process. It went more smoothly than it ever has. I was really wrong to criticize you. You did a great job—and I would like to learn how you put your plan together if you have a chance to teach me sometime." Lynn was absolutely amazed.

Becky is still somewhat difficult. She is occasionally critical. But, because she admitted her critical tendencies to Lynn and gave her credit as she should have, Lynn is more willing to overlook some of Becky's tendencies now. She is still surprised that Becky was so humble, but she is also willing to give Becky more respect. Becky rebuilt some personal credibility with Lynn.

"I Meant Well, but I Blew It!"

Sometimes our mistakes are made out of our best intentions. Still, our personal credibility can be reduced even in those circumstances. "Barbara" assumed a new position as the director of Human Resources with a division of a financial services organization. Prior to joining this organization, Barbara had about ten years of experience with another large organization. In both organizations, coordinating the annual performance evaluation and salary planning process was a part of her role. But, Barbara did not agree with the methods used by her new organization. The system she was accustomed to established performance reviews and pay increase dates based upon the individual employees' original hire dates. For example, if someone was hired in August, that person received a performance review and salary increase in August. As a result of this process, managers conducted employee evaluations and made salary changes *throughout* the calendar year. In her new company, the performance review process for all employees was conducted in December, at year-end, with all salary increases occurring the first pay period of March of the following year.

Barbara recommended that her new company consider moving away from a year-end process. She made a strong case with her corporate leadership staff for making the change. She argued that an anniversary date-driven process would allow managers to spend more quality time assessing the performance of each individual if the process occurred throughout the year. She made the point that salaries could be managed with more thoughtful consideration if the process was not pushed through at year-end. Her ideas were politely considered, but no change occurred. Barbara decided to try making her point again, gathering more financial data to support her argument, which proved that the organization could actually save expenses by spreading the process throughout the year. Still, the organizational leaders decided to stay with their established methods of handling the process.

Barbara believed that her arguments to change the system were ones that the managers she worked with would agree strongly with. She continued her battle, which involved several more meetings with the corporate leadership. In the meantime, the calendar was moving forward. Two months passed while Barbara attempted to change the system—two months of the time that managers should have been preparing performance reviews and making salary recommendations. So, finally accepting the organizational decision, Barbara was required to notify managers in early December of very short turnaround dates for their performance reviews and salary planning process. Managers within the organization were quite upset that they had such a short amount of time to get this work done, and that their time for getting the work done would occur during the holiday period. They were not aware of the reasons for the delay—they only understood that their new Human Resources director was giving them very short notice and little time to accomplish a major task at year-end. Barbara's personal credibility was definitely on the downward slide with her new organization, yet she had only the well-being of her organization's managers at heart!

From Problems to Progress

In our previous examples, both Joe and Becky made mistakes. Both made the type of mistakes that hurt the lives of others around them.

But, both made the decision to acknowledge those mistakes, first to themselves, then with those who had been impacted by their mistakes.

Barbara made mistakes as well, even though she was genuinely trying to do the right thing. The good news is that Barbara was able to rebuild personal credibility with the managers in her organization. What was her process? Yes, it was to take ownership with her managers and gain their involvement. After the year-end performance management process was over, Barbara met with each departmental manager. She began each meeting by stating that she wanted to acknowledge some mistakes she had made with the year-end performance management process. She then shared with them what she had been doing in trying to get the organization to consider a changed process. She ended her statement with, "Regardless of my intent, I should have been much more proactive in my communication with you before the end of the year. I apologize for the results of my effort—even if my intent was a good one. It won't happen again." Every manager who heard this stated that they would strongly support Barbara's recommendation of spreading the performance management process throughout the calendar year. A few managers indicated a willingness to participate in a meeting with the corporate leadership group to discuss the issue again, with hopes of changing the system for the following year. All expressed gratitude for Barbara's efforts of working on their behalf.

What did the managers remember about Barbara? They remembered that she was working hard on their behalf and that she took the initiative to explain her actions. Eventually, the year-end performance review and salary planning process was changed. Most of all, the managers remember that positive change occurred in the end. And, they remembered Barbara's part in getting that done. She was clearly able to turn this situation of her lost credibility into one of strengthened credibility.

chapter thirteen

Rebuilding:
One Step at a Time

Anyone who loses credibility can choose to rebuild it. A few tough steps are necessary, but rebuilding credibility is impossible to do it without first taking the following five steps.

Step 1:
Objectively Acknowledge Your Own Actions

This is the toughest part of the process of rebuilding credibility. It requires that we say, "I messed up" to ourselves. It requires that we stop justifying our actions or making excuses for our shortcomings. It means that we must be able to objectively look at what we have done and accept the fact that we were wrong or made a mistake—even when our intentions were good or when there were extenuating circumstances.

Step 2:
Identify Your Options for the Next Action

After you have acknowledged your actions, you now have a choice for your next action. Your choices almost always include the following:

- I can choose to do nothing.
- I can choose to defend myself for what I have done.
- I can choose to take ownership for mistakes I have made.

Regardless, the option you choose will impact your personal credibility. If you choose to do nothing or to defend yourself, you are choosing to leave your personal credibility in its current state.

Step 3:
Verbally Take Ownership with Those Impacted

If you have made a mistake and you have taken ownership for that within your own mind, you are more than halfway to rebuilding credibility. Now, you just need to swallow that pride and let the right people know that you have accepted ownership of the mistake. You don't need to grovel; you don't need to go overboard. You just need to approach that person and state that you have accepted ownership for this mistake.

"Lynn" was shocked yet pleased when "Becky" initiated the conversation with her and acknowledged that she had been wrong to criticize Lynn. "Joe's" family had no idea where he was until he sought them out and verbally took ownership for his behavior as a father and husband. "Barbara"'s discussion with each departmental manager opened the door to improved organizational processes in the future. None of these events could have occurred without each person's willingness to verbally take ownership with those he or she had impacted.

Step 4:
Manage Your Expectations

If you recall, it took Joe's daughter, "Amy," three years to open her heart and mind to her father. His other daughter, "Carrie," has yet to do that, and might not ever. His former wife was unwilling to consider allowing Joe the opportunity to rebuild credibility with her. Joe made it clear that he had no expectations of being forgiven; he simply knew that he needed to let his family know that he realized he had made very serious mistakes with them. Joe could not establish personal credibility *within himself* if he did not begin with taking ownership of his own actions. Self-respect is the foundation for the personal credibility rebuilding process. Going into the conversations with his family members, Joe set very realistic expectations that his family might not ever forgive him. He needed, however, to begin with forgiving himself.

Or, it is also possible to see almost immediate acceptance and experience increased personal credibility as in the case with "Barbara" and her handling of the performance management process within her organization. The managers she worked with were not happy with how she had managed the year-end process, but after understanding her motives and desires, they were very willing to work with her going forward.

Your expectations for rebuilding credibility will be best managed if you are able to focus on one thing: You.

Do you know that *you have accepted ownership*? Do you know that you have acknowledged and discussed that acceptance with anyone who might have been impacted by your actions? You simply cannot control what others choose to do when you sincerely make the attempt to rebuild credibility. Your control begins and ends with you. Your personal credibility can only begin to be rebuilt with self-respect for your own actions.

Accepting ownership does something wonderful for you as an individual. When you are able to admit your own mistakes, and then follow that with admitting them to others, a heavy burden is lifted from you. Even when others don't accept you with open arms, you are much less likely to activate your invisible fence. Your mind says, "Well, I've admitted I was wrong. I can't really do anything else. So, I have no need to keep that fence up and protect myself from anything at this point." Your ability to move forward, forgive yourself, and learn from the entire experience is significantly greater. You are more likely to be open and authentic going forward. And, as we have discussed, you are much more likely to increase personal credibility with others as a result.

146

Step 5:
Share What You Learn from the Rebuilding Process

No matter what, we learn from the process of rebuilding personal credibility. Whenever you can, share your story about how you lost credibility and worked at rebuilding it. Help others see that admitting and owning mistakes is possible—and often leads to amazing results. Be open in talking about your own human mistakes and failures and how taking ownership is the best way to lighten the weight of the baggage these mistakes or failures leave behind! One of the most powerful and effective ways we have to leave a positive impact on others is in sharing our mistakes and what we learned from them.

Starting Over...Every Day

Personal credibility is built, lost, and then rebuilt by most of us on a daily basis. The reality is that no one is ever 100% constantly and totally a credible human being. We are human, with imperfections and failures. When we honestly assess ourselves, our actions, and make decisions to work on changing actions that impact our credibility, we begin immediately tapping into the amazing exponential power of our personal credibility factor. The tough part is that the work really never ends. But, again, neither do the rewards! So, what do we really need to do to get going? Well, we need to start over!

Starting over begins with making a decision to learn from your past mistakes, but also to forgive your own past.

Nothing is accomplished from getting hung up on how "dumb" we have been, or how "horrible" our actions were. The only thing that can be done about the past is to work in the present to change the future. Instead of being hung up, simply ask: What have I learned? What will I change? Then, begin the change process.

Tapping Into the Power of the Three Secrets to Personal Credibility

Learning secrets to gaining personal credibility is helpful. However, it is what we *do* with the knowledge of these secrets that will determine their value on our lives and others around us. As you review the following secrets, take advantage of the opportunity to be completely honest with yourself. Look for opportunities to use these secrets to enhance your personal credibility factor.

Secret #1: Forget Power, Position, Status, and Other Such Nonsense

How important is power, position, and status to you? How much do you over-rely on "because I said so" to accomplish results? How likely are you to give respect to others regardless of their power or position? Where and with whom do you need to focus your actions?

_____

_____

_____

_____

Secret #2: I Can See Right Through You

How totally authentic are you when interacting with others? Are you comfortable in your own skin and allow those around you to see and know the person you really are? Or, do you only allow others to see and know the person you want others to believe you are? How frequently do you activate your "invisible fence" and why do you do it? How might you totally deactivate that invisible fence?

_____

_____

_____

_____

Secret #3: The Decision to Suspend Judgment

How capable are you of putting your own thoughts "on hold" while you consider what you are hearing or learning from others? How capable are you of remaining quiet, open minded, and objective while considering another person's point of view? With whom and when might you most benefit from making the decision to suspend judgment?

_____

_____

_____

_____

Stepping Up with Credibility:
Seven Steps Everyone Can Take to Increase Personal Credibility and Impact

You should be ready at this point to get very specific about your Personal Credibility Factor Action Plan. For best results, go back and reflect on your notes in previous chapters. Review your observations about your opportunities with tapping into the Three Secrets. You are now ready to prepare for action!

In the spaces provided in the following sections, list at least one action step that you will take to increase your personal credibility. There are spaces provided for two specific actions in each step. Caution: Don't overwhelm yourself. Start by deciding which of the seven steps are more challenging for you and where your actions would create the most positive impact on your personal credibility. Work first on those areas, and then revisit your list on occasion, perhaps monthly. Remember to set expectations for yourself and others realistically. Always remember, we get to start over every day!

Step #1: Know Your "Stuff"

1. I will:

   _____

   _____

2. I will:

   _____

   _____

Step #2: Keep Commitments

1.   I will:

_____

_____

2.   I will:

_____

_____

Step #3: Honor Confidences and Avoid Gossip

1.   I will:

_____

_____

2.   I will:

_____

_____

Step #4: Know Yourself—the Good, the Bad, and the Ugly!

1.   I will:

_____

_____

2.   I will:

_____

_____

Step #5: Choose to Value Others—the Good, and Yes, Even the Bad and the Ugly!

1. I will:

   _____

   _____

2. I will:

   _____

   _____

Step #6: Ask More and Listen Most

1. I will:

   _____

   _____

2. I will:

   _____

   _____

Step #7: Create Credible Interactions

1. I will:

   _____

   _____

2. I will:

   _____

   _____

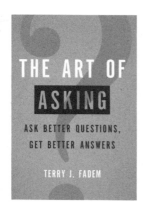

FT Press

The Art of Asking: Ask Better Questions, Get Better Answers

Terry J. Fadem

0137144245 / 9780137144242
Available now

Read the following excerpt from
The Art of Asking to...

It's not enough to ask questions; you must ask the right questions in the best way possible. Use questions to promote innovation, drive change, identify hidden problems, and get failing projects back on track.

That means asking the *right* questions in the *right* ways. This book will teach you how to do precisely that. Terry J. Fadem shows how to choose the right questions and avoid questions that guarantee obvious, useless answers...how to help people give you the information you need...how to use body language to ask questions more effectively...how to ask the innovative or neglected questions that uncover real issues and solutions.

You'll learn how to adopt the attributes of a good questioner...set a goal for every question...use your personal style more effectively...ask tough questions, elicit dissent, react to surprises, overcome evasions, and more. Becoming a better questioner may be the most powerful thing you can do right now to improve your managerial effectiveness—and this book gives you all the insights, tools, and techniques you'll need to get there.

Introduction: Questioning Is the Skill of Management

1. Is There a Basic Set of Management Questions?

Yes.

All managers can use a basic set of questions, at any level in any organization, in any situation, anywhere in the world, and in any language. These questions are tools that should be issued to each manager when he or she joins the profession. Most professionals have a basic set of implements to use in their craft. Carpenters have hammers, dentists have picks, and physicians have stethoscopes. It is hard to envision any of these people working in their chosen fields without their basic set of tools. Managers, too, have a basic set of tools: *questions.* And nothing is as simple, or as complex, for a manager, or for any person in any position of authority and responsibility, than asking questions.

Some of us are very good at it. We always seem to ask the right question at the right time. Others of us are less well prepared, and our questions often do not yield the kinds of results we want or that the business needs. Even the best among us are subject to a number of common errors. So, all of us managers share the need to improve our skills. Before we start discussing the details of common questioning errors, a quick review of the basic tools of management is provided.

If you want the basics, the following list should suffice. There is a lot more to asking a question than merely using an interrogative, but these words do cover the full managerial spectrum of interrogation.

Basic Questions

For all managers in any situation at any time

What?

Where?

When?

Why?

Who?

How?

How much?

What if?[1]

These questions are universally applicable. If you are ever in a situation where you need a question, or if you want to make certain all questions have been asked, just run down the list. This list also serves as a handy checklist when you need to make a quick decision. Consider which of the issues implied by these interrogative words have not been addressed in the situation you are facing, and then raise those issues.

This list happens to be my personal shorthand way of making certain I have covered all perspectives in a discussion. You can add a number of other questioning words and phrases. Words such as *which*, *is*, *could*, *would*, *should*, *do*, *can*, *will*, and so on are used every day and could be the basis for another list. It all depends on what you expect to accomplish.

Organizations need all their managers to be successful, not just the ones who ultimately end up in the executive suite. The purpose of focusing on improving the quality of questions is to improve the quality of management, all management.

Success does not necessarily follow the ability to ask questions. It rests on the confluence of a lot of variables. However, by spending time considering how to improve a basic management skill—questioning—the outcome should certainly be better than what it would have been otherwise.

Could any of the well-known corporate disasters of our day have been avoided with better questions, asked more often by more people, such as the boards of these companies? We will never know. However, by improving questioning skills among more managers in a business, chances are good that other disasters can be averted in the future.

You can use the monosyllabic queries previously listed, if you choose, or you can work on developing questioning as a skill. Either way, the purpose of this book is to influence managers to think about questioning differently. In addition to the basic list of questions, you can use the accompanying rules to improve the act of asking a question.

Try these ten simple rules. Their use will help improve the clarity of your communication.

Ten Basic Rules for Asking Questions

1. Be direct.
2. Make eye contact if asking the question in person.
3. Use plain language.
4. Use simple sentence structure.
5. Be brief.
6. Maintain focus on the subject at hand.
7. Make certain the purpose of the question is clear.
8. The question must be appropriate for the situation and the person.
9. The manner/of asking should reflect the intent.
10. Know what to do with the answer.

2. Asking Questions Is the Skill of Effective Management

Managers do not need answers to operate a successful business; they need questions. Answers can come from anyone, anytime, anywhere in the world thanks to the benefits of all the electronic communication tools at our disposal.

This has turned the real job of management into determining what it is the business needs to know, along with the *who/what/where/when* and *how* of learning it. To effectively solve problems, seize opportunities, and achieve objectives, questions need to be asked by managers—these are the people responsible for the operation of the enterprise as a whole.

All questions asked in a business setting are asked within the context of organizational expectations. This context is the "expectations of success" context in which all corporate discussions are conducted. I have yet to find a business that is seeking anything other than success, however it is they choose to define it.

This context of expectations defines the box that business people "think in." Success is specifically defined by the function, such as sales or research, or by the market, but the box frames the questions for each specific inquiry— or, in some cases, the *inquisition.*

Expectations of Success

QUESTIONS + ANSWERS = SUCCESS

The inquiry process is characterized as a linear model, and for our purposes of this discussion, it is linear. All the divergent thinking, outside-the-box thinking, or any other paths people may follow move along this general line—from questions to answers to results.

The process of asking a question within this context has eight basic elements:

1. What do we know?
2. What do we not know?
3. What are our objectives?
4. What do we need to know now to reach our objectives?
5. Who are we going to learn this from?
6. How are we going to learn it?
7. What are the expected results from deploying what is learned?
8. What do we do as a result of learning the answer?

This is the basic process along which questioning proceeds. Elegant models can be added to improve any aspect of inquiry a business might need. However, the focus remains the same, it remains simple, and it remains defined as success. If more success is desired, ask more questions. If the business wants to pursue a new business model, build a new box of expectations.

3. How Good Are Your Skills?

The numbers of brain workers, or nonproducers, as they are called,
should be as small as possible in proportion to the numbers of
workers, i.e., those who actually work....

—*Fredrick Winslow Taylor,[2] father of modern management*

"Brain workers" was the original concept of scientific management pioneered by Fredrick Winslow Taylor. His theories produced the foundation for management portrayed as "modern" in the twentieth century. Think about how much has changed over time. Brain workers are now the producers in today's world of business.

Historically, managers possessed the knowledge, experience, and skills necessary to perform the tasks relevant to the daily operation of the business. They could function as both bosses and employees. This competency was the primary reason business owners promoted their employees to management. The complex needs of the modern business have changed this model.

Such diverse knowledge is now required in business that an individual manager is rarely expected to be knowledgeable enough to run all aspects of the business successfully without employee specialists. So, what do generalist managers have to know to maintain the progress of their enterprise? *They must know how to ask questions.*

How Good Are Your Questioning Skills?

While I was traveling around the world on a business assignment that I discuss later in this chapter, I noticed that many managers asked similar questions and got amazingly different results. The way questions were asked appeared to be as important as the question itself. I looked around for a book to serve as a good training guide for myself on how to ask questions. The resources I found fell into two categories: professional training guides (such as for lawyers, teachers, and market researchers) and self-help books designed to enable the individual to get ahead (such as with interviewing skills, or improving a person's thinking processes). These are all excellent resources. A number of them are referenced later. However, my goal was to find a basic skills book. I was unable to find one that met my criteria.

When I started studying questions, I started with the assumption that I knew nothing about them. So, I built this book as a personal reference because I was unable to find what I needed.

After I embraced my own ignorance about questioning, I started to see questions in a new light. I found that even experienced, successful managers run into problems with their questions on occasion. They fall into traps such as habit questioning, posturing, or putting answers in their questions. Other managers, particularly new ones, commit a number of errors, such as asking prejudicial questions or leveling complex questions about interesting but unimportant or even unrelated details. Fixing these mistakes early in a person's career can lead to better personal performance over time. Fixing them among all managers can often lead to improved business performance.

The bottom line for all of us is that we need good questions because we want better answers. There was a need, at some point, at Enron, for example, for someone to ask the tough questions—*inquisitor's questions.* Investors needed someone to ask serious questions of the people at Global Crossing and at many other firms where damage occurred. It is not the job of any government agency to clean up these messes by asking business questions; that is the responsibility of management. *Management* is an inclusive word to mean anyone in a position of authority/responsibility—from line supervisors to board members.

Lives and careers have been ruined, not by questions, but by the lack of questions. As managers, we either do not know how to ask, what to ask, or are unable to ask the question for a variety of reasons. Sometimes we avoid certain questions because we believe that by asking them we risk our job, our status, personal embarrassment, or perhaps we are just being polite.

If managers at all levels were empowered by improved skills to ask questions sooner, better, and with an eye on what is best for the business or for their organization, disasters could be reduced and in some cases perhaps avoided altogether.

Management needs questions before it gets answers.

4. You Ask Too Many Questions

A downside to questioning should be explained: It is possible to ask too many questions, to ask them at the wrong time, or to completely misunderstand your situation; in many cases, the mere act of asking questions can even cost you your job.

• ⚙ •

A young business division of a major corporation[3] was poised to introduce a new product, something the parent company had done, literally, a thousand times before. Only this time, a problem existed. Simply put, the product did not work. To make matters worse, no one appeared to be aware of this.

Was management blinded by the potential earnings from a product with a large gross margin? Perhaps it was the rush to get to market before the competition that caused such denial. Or was research, or manufacturing, or some other part of the company covering up the problem?

The situation came to a head about a week before the scheduled commercial launch.

Not a single person in management was aware of any problems. Everyone was focusing on the expected outcome—a boost in sales with a significant increase in earnings. The prospective new product had a large gross margin, and no competitive products were on the horizon. These kinds of opportunities do not come along every day, so all management eyes were on this product, this team, and the numbers.

The scene where the first inkling of a problem occurred was at the product team meeting. A half-dozen people were gathered in a small conference room at the divisional headquarters. They were conducting a rather perfunctory review of all aspects of the new product: technical development, manufacturing, marketing, sales, and service. The development process for this product had been flawless.

A massive report containing all relevant information sat in front of each person. The oversized notebook contained the marketing plan, manufacturing reports, technical service plans, global distribution plans, and a voluminous section filled with quality-control testing data.

Manufacturing was churning out inventory in anticipation of a worldwide release while the sales force was being trained on product benefits. Advertising and marketing materials were already distributed globally in a dozen different languages. All distribution plans had been checked and rechecked in preparation. This was all standard procedure in the company.

Everything had gone smoothly for the first-time product manager (PM) who was chairing this meeting. She eagerly anticipated the success of this product as a "career maker." It had all the attributes that PMs dream of: large market demand, lack of competitive products, high projected earnings, low costs, and an experienced support team to help get her over any rough spots that might occur. Up to this point, it was smooth sailing.

Most of her team were old hands; the manufacturing superintendent and the technical development manager were both 20-year veterans, and the quality-control manager was a professional quality engineer (QE) and had participated in dozens of product releases. A just-hired technical-support person was the final member of the team. He was to be responsible for managing the technical service effort that would support customers after they purchased the product. He had been on the job all of one week, after a month of orientation training.

According to company procedures, all members of the product team were required to sign the product release form before any new product could ship. Even the newly hired person would be required to sign—company policy mandated that he be considered a full member of the team, with the same responsibilities as all other team members in the review and release of product. After all, he was to manage the support of the product after it was released into customer hands, so his was a key role in the process.

Following a brief review of quality-control testing data, the new guy starts to ask some questions.

New guy (interrupting the meeting to ask an obvious and somewhat foolish question): I noticed that all the numbers on the final testing chart are at the lowest possible limit for an acceptable release of product to customers. Am I reading this correctly?

Technical manager: Where did you say you went to school? (followed by laughter)

QE (mocking the new guy): Yes. So what?

New guy: May I see the raw data from the testing lab?

Manufacturing superintendent (pissed off by this young, inexperienced, ignorant new employee): We do not have time for this BS!

Technical manager (acting highly insulted): Listen. As you can see, the data shows that the numbers are still all in the range of acceptable performance.

New guy (unaware that he is a major irritant to everyone in the room): That may be so, but the question I am really asking is have these numbers been rounded?

Quality-control manager (angered by the assertion that the data was somehow tainted): Yes, and all of it has been done correctly and according to proper scientific notation! You do have a degree, don't you? (more laughter)

New guy (undaunted by his obvious ignorance): How many product samples were tested?

Quality-control manager (annoyed and red-faced): Testing was performed on samples taken randomly from production inventory according to proper procedure. For college graduates, this means that the numbers are statistically relevant.

New guy (continuing to question the group, although he is by now conscious of the rising stress levels in the room caused by his questions): Although the data is scientifically correct, did any single sample of the product pass all five tests by more than the minimum?

Quality-control manager: Why you arrogant bastard!

Technical manager: Do you think we are stupid? There are well over 50 years of experience in this room, and what do you know after being on the job for 1 week?

New guy (now aware that he has a problem): The numbers we are using to pass the product for release represent a potential problem. They are all low. As a matter of fact, if the testing was as tight as the data suggests, then do you think that any of this product is any good?

PM (wanting to avoid a meltdown of her first product team): Time for a break. Let's all get some coffee and reconvene in about 10 minutes.

Collectively, the members of this product team were responsible for a consistent run of profitable new products without encountering any major problems in the market. They had complete confidence in each other and credibility with corporate officers.

The technical and manufacturing leaders escorted the new guy to the coffeepot. Many man-years and millions of dollars had been invested in this product. In addition, their personal reputations were at stake.

These senior managers were not about to allow this newly hired outsider to get in the way of their personal string of successful product releases. Their annual bonus and future compensation rested on these new products, which, at this point in their careers, represented a significant amount of money. They had seen similar situations before where products barely made it through testing but were acceptable in the market. The company was a market leader known for quality products. So, the test data came as no surprise to them.

Even if a problem existed, they knew it would be fixed as quickly as it was discovered. As a matter of fact, that was the role of the new guy. His job was to support this product once it reached the market. They did not take a liking to him.

The hallway discussion was over quickly.

> **Manufacturing superintendent:** You were assigned to this team to keep your mouth shut and learn. We do not think you are going to work out here. You ask too many questions. You should look for employment elsewhere.

And with that dismissal, the technical manager and the manufacturing superintendent walked back into the meeting room.

As the new guy was returning to his office, his boss (summoned by the PM, who wanted to avoid a nasty scene) met him in the hallway. Effective immediately, the new guy was put on a temporary assignment.

However, now uncertain about the results, the PM nervously reconvened the team without the "new guy." She was upset. This person whom she had never met before raised doubts in her mind that she could not dismiss as easily as her team members had sent the new guy packing. She elected to put off the final signing, on a technicality, to allow another customer technical-support person to be placed on the team. This proved to be a wise decision.

The product was never released. It did not work, just like the new guy had suggested after questioning the data. However, the business continued to persist in the development of this product because it was high on the wish list of their customers and the earning potential was greater than any other new product planned for the next two years. The invested dollars produced nothing of value. The product never went to market.

•☉•

This is the story of how I started my career in industry. My reassignment, my punishment for saving the company from a serious problem, was to fly all over the world investigating and resolving customer product-quality complaints. I was to visit each and every site where customers had product-quality complaints that could not be verified in any way by normal procedures and resolve the problem.

I decided to accept the situation. How could I explain a painfully short tenure on my resumé? So, I was on the road (or in the sky) almost every day for nearly a year.

I was completely unequipped for this assignment. I was responsible for customers, and I was empowered to act as their agent. But, I thought this meant very little. I had no influence with anyone at the company. My immediate supervisor and the managers at the next level wanted me to quit and were doing everything possible to encourage me to find another job (so that they wouldn't have to fire me and run the risk of exposing their product problems). In spite of this, I discovered that I was able to have a significant impact on the company.

I found that I could help solve problems, reduce the number of customer complaints, improve products, and even increase revenue by asking questions. When I called back to the company on behalf of a customer, I questioned everybody and anybody about product quality. I had no problem calling the plant manager, the fascist superintendent who tried to intimidate me into quitting, or anyone else to solve problems for customers—my customers. I was prosecutor, inquisitor, and chief justice of the court of customer confidence.

After all, they had already fired me! I had little interest in the usual politics or politeness that normally gets people promoted out of such awful assignments. The only threat that the company held over me was to stop depositing money into my checking account. Although I knew that day would inevitably arrive, I was on a mission.

It was on this extended journey that I started to recognize the value of questions. Questions got actions. Questions also resulted in more questions. Questions caused people to think. Questions also made people uncomfortable, created stress, and could cause problems of their own.

I asked questions. I listened to the questions others asked in response to my questions. I listened to customers' questions.

Then, I started to keep notes on the "good" questions until I also realized that almost any question had the potential of having a positive or negative impact (often depending on who was asking and how). I also started to observe what managers said and how managers communicated when they asked questions.

The PM and I became reacquainted when I finally returned to the home office. She shared with me how upset she was by what happened in the project meeting. My questions had raised concerns in her mind that were just not there before I naively opened my mouth. Her instincts told her to be worried not only about the product, but also about the team she was running (and to be concerned about her career). She was on the fast track to be promoted before this bump in the road.

I had stumbled into her project meeting like some kind of drunk, spewing questions without concern for how my behavior might affect others. My questions may have been good ones—and it was clear that my insights were correct—but my approach left a lot to be desired. Our conversation went something like this:

> **PM:** They laughed a lot after you left the meeting. I felt like crying. After you raised doubts, I had to follow up, and you know the rest. You do know that my boss is the manufacturing superintendent's wife?

I was dumbstruck. It had not occurred to me that personal as well as professional relationships dot the landscape of businesses. My inexperience had contributed to a near-fatal career event for a talented businesswoman.

> **Me:** After I started to ask questions, to follow the trail, I just did not know how to stop. Also, I knew that even if I said nothing, I would not have signed that release authorization.

> **PM:** Well, at the time, I thought my career was over. But if we had let that product out, I would have been blamed for the whole mess anyway and might not have had a job to worry about. So, I did what a product manager is supposed to do—more teams and more meetings. I will get another project, but you had better watch your back.[4]

Her stressful experience, as a result of being on the other side of my questions, sensitized me to understand that I needed to fully appreciate the context, both personal and professional, as much as possible when asking questions.

·◉·

Some managers were good at asking questions. Through insight, habit, or inquisitiveness, they made a positive impact on their businesses—on the people in their organizations. As I observed the management practices of both effective and ineffective managers, I started to break things down into bite-sized chunks for ease of use for me as a reference.

When I finally did reach management positions, I found this resource to be an invaluable guide. As I started to work more closely with leaders of one company, and then with leaders of other companies, I studied their questions, how they asked them, and what kinds of results they achieved.

This book is a distillation of those observations along with an analysis of questions as a management tool.

> If managers are looking for better answers, they must start by improving their questioning.
>
>

FINANCIAL TIMES

In an increasingly competitive world, it is quality
of thinking that gives an edge—an idea that opens new
doors, a technique that solves a problem, or an insight
that simply helps make sense of it all.

We work with leading authors in the various arenas
of business and finance to bring cutting-edge thinking
and best-learning practices to a global market.

It is our goal to create world-class print publications
and electronic products that give readers
knowledge and understanding that can then be
applied, whether studying or at work.

To find out more about our business
products, you can visit us at www.ftpress.com.